# ALMOST HUMAN

# ALMOST HUMAN

The Astonishing Tale of *Homo naledi* and the
Discovery That Changed Our Human Story

## LEE BERGER
### AND JOHN HAWKS

NATIONAL GEOGRAPHIC
Washington, D.C.

Published by National Geographic Partners, LLC
1145 17th Street NW Washington, DC 20036

ISBN: 978-1-4262-1811-8

Since 1888, the National Geographic Society has funded more than 12,000 research, exploration, and preservation projects around the world. National Geographic Partners distributes a portion of the funds it receives from your purchase to National Geographic Society to support programs including the conservation of animals and their habitats.

National Geographic Partners
1145 17th Street NW
Washington, DC 20036-4688 USA

Become a member of National Geographic and activate your benefits today at natgeo.com/jointoday.

For information about special discounts for bulk purchases, please contact National Geographic Books Special Sales: specialsales@natgeo.com

For rights or permissions inquiries, please contact National Geographic Books Subsidiary Rights: bookrights@natgeo.com

*Interior design: Nicole Miller*

Printed in the United States of America

17/QGF-LSCML/1

To our families, for their support during
the course of this remarkable journey, and to the
entire team, for making the journey possible.

# KEY SITES IN THE SEARCH
# FOR HUMAN ORIGINS

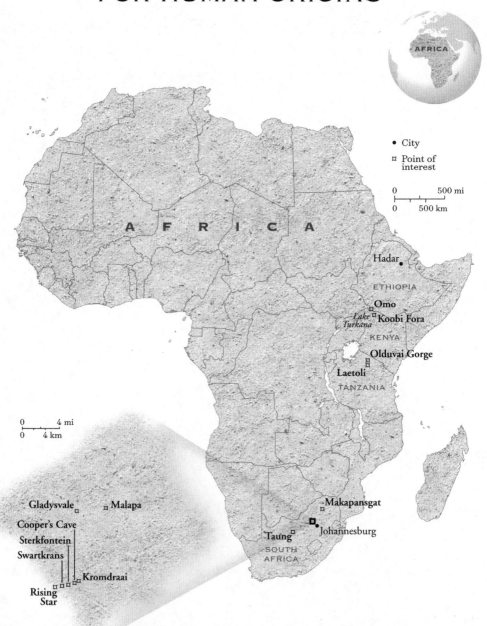

AFRICA

● City
▫ Point of interest

0 —— 500 mi
0 —— 500 km

A F R I C A

Hadar ●

ETHIOPIA

Omo
Lake
Turkana
Koobi Fora

KENYA

Olduvai Gorge

Laetoli

TANZANIA

0 —— 4 mi
0 —— 4 km

Gladysvale      ▫ Malapa

Cooper's Cave

Sterkfontein

Swartkrans

Kromdraai

Rising
Star

Makapansgat

Taung      Johannesburg

SOUTH
AFRICA

# CRADLE OF HUMANKIND
## A UNESCO WORLD HERITAGE SITE

# CONTENTS

❧

# ALMOST
# HUMAN

# PROLOGUE

Slipping between the loose, rusty wires of the game fence, I paused to let my son, Matthew, through. I pressed my foot down on the lowest wire, pushing just hard enough to create a gap for Matt and my young Rhodesian ridgeback, Tau. I'd barely made much of a space before they darted through.

With me on the other side was Job Kibii, a slim, Kenyan paleoanthropology postdoctoral student; we both smiled at our companions' youthful energy. I pulled the wires wider for Job, and we turned toward a small cluster of wild olives and white stinkwood trees. Matt and Tau were already in the trees' shade, a few dozen meters away.

"That's it," I said, gesturing toward the ring of trees. "I can't believe I didn't find it earlier."

Job nodded in agreement as he surveyed the rolling landscape of the Cradle of Humankind. The Cradle, a large area designated by UNESCO as a World Heritage site, is not far from my home in Johannesburg, South Africa. Just a few dozen kilometers outside a metropolis of more than five million people, this place is a world away: a pristine wilderness, home to zebras, antelopes, giraffes—even leopards and hyenas. It is also one of the most famous areas for fossil discovery on the planet. Most of that fame was established during a golden age of paleoanthropology, from the mid-1930s up to the 1970s, when scientists discovered caves full of fossil bone deposits going back three million years.

I had known this area for 18 years; for the past several months, I had been conducting a new survey of fossil sites here. It was the morning of August 15, 2008—a typical winter morning on the Highveld: crisp, cool, and cloudless. I had no idea that in just a few minutes, my life was going to change forever, thanks to a discovery made by a boy and a dog.

ᘒ

I WAS WORKING TO confirm a hunch, originating with a 10-year-old computer error that had set me in motion a few months before. The previous December, I had started surveying this terrain I knew so well with Google Earth, the new satellite image–viewing software. Of course, the first thing I looked at was my house (where, thank goodness, the satellite hadn't caught me lounging by the pool). Then I checked the sites I already knew. Google Earth was new, but I had been surveying the Cradle using handheld global positioning system (GPS) units since 1998. I could practically recite the lat-long positions for fossil sites from memory.

I started with Gladysvale, a cave situated nearly in the center of the Cradle where I had first worked in 1991 and where I had found two hominin teeth. Hominins—also called hominids—are members of the human family tree, which includes all the extinct species more closely related to people than to any great apes living today. Hominin bones are precious pieces of evidence for our origins.

I had expected we would find more hidden treasures among the tons of rock and sediment we excavated during the next decade and a half of exploration at Gladysvale. But in the long run, although my colleagues, students, and I found the remains of thousands upon thousands of antelopes, we found only fragments of one or two hominins. Still, I loved the place, loved the feeling of being in the bush. I had even loved looking at every one of those antelope bones, even if they weren't from hominins.

With Google Earth up on my computer screen, I punched in Gladysvale's GPS coordinates. I remember seeing the satellite image leap upward from my house, way up into the sky, swing northwest, and then rapidly zoom down onto the Cradle. I could see the familiar hills, streams, and valleys around Gladysvale becoming sharper and sharper. But as the image blurred to huge pixels, I saw there was something wrong. This wasn't Gladysvale: It was actually the valley next to Gladysvale—a spot almost 300 meters away! I typed in the coordinates of another place I had worked, the Cooper's Cave site. Again, the image leaped into the air, this time moving southwest. Again, the position was wrong. I entered location after location, and none was correct. I was horrified. Had I recorded the GPS coordinates incorrectly? Had I been working with the wrong numbers for almost a decade?

I soon learned that in the 1990s, before GPS was perfected for public use, the handheld units were primitive and somewhat error-prone—in part because they were designed for military use, with deliberate error built in to confound potential enemies. It meant that to use Google Earth to view all those sites I knew—more than 130 altogether—I had to relocate their positions manually.

That left me trawling the landscape on the computer screen. At first I felt frustrated—years of work had to be corrected—but slowly I began to recognize that this mistake was leading me to a new way of looking at things. I began to understand what caves and fossil sites really looked like from overhead. Some were marked by clusters of trees, some by disturbances in the ground. Sometimes they were clustered, often in linear patterns that I realized must mark the geological faults that had allowed caves to form. Slowly the prospect emerged that the Cradle of Humankind might contain more sites than anyone had previously thought: in the bedrock, underground.

The bedrock underlying the quarter million hectares of Cradle land is made up of dolomitic limestone. Extremely hard and resistant to erosion, it makes a rocky land surface with outcrops, cliffs, and exposed areas of rock that slowly weather in a pattern that the locals call "elephant skin rock." Cracks and faults within the dolomite allow water to seep downward, dissolving the rock and creating cavities and fissures over millions of years. Through those millennia, animals have used those caves, sometimes leaving bones—their own bones or those of their prey. As the water percolates through, these bones can get stuck together with gravel, dirt, and rocks, resulting in a jumbled, cemented mass of fossil bone and rock called breccia. The breccias of the Cradle have given rise to many of the world's most important fossil discoveries relating to human evolution.

In February 2008, I had begun to verify my hunch about undiscovered sites, ground-truthing the idea by good old-fashioned walking. As I did the footwork, I found that about one in 10 sites held something worth mapping: pretty good odds in the fossil-finding business. By July 2008, I had discovered almost 600 previously unrecognized cave and fossil sites—and this in the most explored area on Earth for these types of sites!

The site that Matt, Job, and I were exploring that August day in 2008 was one I had settled on two weeks earlier. What drew me to it was a grove of trees: Wild olive and white stinkwood trees had become my new guide to the Cradle geology. These species often grow near cave openings, I had come to realize, because cracks in the dolomite allow water to penetrate deep into the rock, creating a pathway for the trees' roots through the water-starved dry season.

This grove of trees looked no different from the others. It was right near a road I had driven hundreds of times before. But there was an old miners' track that I had somehow missed, and that predicted a cave nearby. Miners around here wouldn't have been looking for gold. They would have been finding limestone-rich caves, blasting out deposits of calcite rock, and baking it in kilns to produce quicklime, which is then used to make concrete and extract gold from ore found elsewhere in South Africa. The lime miners had worked the landscape extensively, but more recently I'd combed it ceaselessly for fossils. I had hiked over practically every inch of it in those years—it was a place I loved, a place that had been my laboratory for much of my research. I knew it probably better than anyone alive.

We were just over the hill from Gladysvale, the cave where I had tried—and so far, failed—to make a big hominin find. Over the years, I had looked at hundreds of little fossil sites like this one, turning over rocks and examining the small cross sections of broken fossil bones sticking out of them. Now, standing in front of yet another potential site, I didn't get my hopes up, but I was always ready to explore. "Shall we take a look?" I asked, tilting the brim of my hat back. It was a rhetorical question—seeing what this little site might have to offer was why we were there.

Walking toward the grove of trees, I kept my eyes on the ground, scanning for any anomaly different from the native rock. Tiny white chips of lime were scattered about, marking the miners' trackway like breadcrumbs in a fairy tale. Large blocks of breccia lay by the track, blasted out and then tossed aside. We passed more and more of them as we approached the main pit left behind by the mining operation. I picked up a rock about the size of a basketball and gestured to Job to come take a look. Matthew and Tau looked on curiously.

"This is the first one I found." I turned the rock so Job and Matt could see. My fingers traced an orange bone embedded in chocolate brown rock.

"An antelope metapodial?" asked Job.

I nodded. It was the fossilized leg bone of an antelope. Job was an expert in fauna—animals and their fossil bones—and had come with me that morning to decide whether this deposit would contribute to his own research.

"They are always antelopes," I said, shaking my head with a grin. So many antelopes, so few hominins.

I knew people who had made big discoveries—discoveries that had struck their worlds like lightning. I wasn't one of those people. Still, I counted myself lucky. At age 42, I was a successful scientist with a very good run of fieldwork and research papers. Over 19 years of searching, I had found maybe a dozen bits and pieces of hominin fossils among thousands of other animal fossils.

Paleoanthropology—the search for human origins—is a tough, competitive, and unforgiving field. A colleague of mine once joked that we are probably the only branch of science that has more scientists than objects to study. That wasn't too far from the truth. In a field of such scarcity, even a small find—a jawbone, even a single leg bone—could make a career.

But now, as we stood at the edge of the pit, I had my doubts about the quality of this site. For one thing, it was too small—nothing like the big sites of the Cradle that had yielded the important hominin fossils. The odds were tiny. Maybe one in hundreds of thousands of fossils will be a hominin bone, and so you need a lot of fossils to start. This tiny pit couldn't possibly contain many thousands of fossils, and so it wasn't a very good bet. But Matt was eager, so I was willing.

The miners' work had been hasty. Marks on the walls of the pit indicated where they had put in dynamite charges, blasting out brown chunks of breccia with angular, freshly broken edges, scattered under and around the trees. The miners hadn't put very much effort into digging here. They left only a handful of blast holes before moving farther up the valley.

"OK, go find fossils," I said to Job and Matt. "If you find anything, let me know. We'll see what this site has to offer."

Matt and Tau bounded off into the high grass away from the pit. I imagined that they had decided to chase antelopes instead of hunting fossils today. I smiled as I watched them run off, Tau in the lead.

"I think the miners might have been just blasting to get material to pack the road," I said to Job. I gestured to the smaller fragments that seemed deliberately placed among the rougher bedrock of the trackway. "It doesn't look like there was enough lime for them to stay here very long."

Matthew's voice rang out.

"Dad, I found a fossil!"

He was some 20 meters away, over in the tall grass, where there couldn't possibly be any fossils. I glanced over at Job and shrugged. "Let me go see what he's got," I said.

Matt was kneeling next to a broken tree stump. A jagged, charred hole showed where lightning had once struck it. He was holding a rock about the size of a rugby ball. He looked toward me, beaming. Tau was lying down beside him, panting, ears perking as I walked over.

Matt was too far off the site, too far away from that pit, to have found anything very important. Even if it was a fossil, it was probably just a piece of antelope. But he was my nine-year-old son, and I had always encouraged curiosity—and an eagerness to go fossil hunting—in both Matt and my daughter, Megan.

Five meters away, my eyes focused on Matt's rock, and I felt time stop.

Sometimes people who have been in a car crash describe their memory of the event as being like a black-and-white silent movie. That's the way I remember that moment now. A bone stuck out of the rock. I knew instantly what it was: the clavicle, or collarbone, of a hominin. I knew that fossil shape—I had done my Ph.D. research on this bone. Still, I doubted myself. But as I took the rock from Matt and stared at the little S-shaped piece of bone, I thought, "What else could it be?"

I turned the rock over to get a better angle. There was a hominin canine tooth and part of the jaw, as well as other bones. This was not just any hominin. And, at the very least, there were several parts of the skeleton embedded in this chunk of rock.

Matt says I cursed. I don't remember. Whatever I said or did, I knew for sure that both his life and mine were about to change forever.

# PART I
# GOING TO
# SOUTH AFRICA

❧

# 1

I've been rummaging in the dirt, looking for connections to the past, for as long as I can remember.

When I was nine years old, my family lived on a little farm outside Sylvania, Georgia. My greatest love was the outdoors. I spent my afternoons and summers in the woods, swimming in creeks and ponds, searching plowed fields for artifacts, and generally having a good time. I was living a rural kid's dream.

My first memory of archaeology comes from those days. Crossing a plowed field, I came across an arrowhead. Taking this treasure back home, I showed it to my father that evening and he explained its origins to me. He pulled out a Time Life book on American Indians and let me loose on the whole series. The idea that people had lived here long ago, making weapons out of stone, fascinated me. Like most boys my age, I loved dinosaurs and had a dinosaur poster on my bedroom wall. But this arrowhead was something else—something in my own backyard—something that I could find. Finding ancient things became an obsession of mine.

My mother's father was proudly Irish and proudly southern—and as an amateur genealogist, he had worked out the pedigree for both. He would talk to me for hours about our family's roots. My father's father, Grandpa Berger, was a wildcatter: a man who sank wells on speculation to prospect for new oil fields. He combed West Texas for the big strike that never quite came, costing him some fingers in the spinning chains of the drills. Grandma Berger flew light planes and had a pet chimpanzee, among other eccentricities. They were risktakers, those two, and my father told stories about growing up in the slipstream trailer pulled behind the latest model Cadillac.

Growing up this way, my father had never really settled in one place. He attended both Texas A&M and the University of Arkansas, where he met my mother. She was a teacher, like her parents; he entered the corporate world of insurance. After having my older brother, Lamont, they moved to Shawnee Mission, Kansas, where I was born. Our family followed my father's work for a few years, from Kansas to Connecticut and then to Georgia, where he worked for a regional insurance company.

In true 1970s style, my parents tried their hand at raising our own food, which meant chickens, a few cows, and a menagerie of other small farm animals. Our old farmhouse outside Sylvania was built of pine, raised off the ground on bricks for cooling in the summer heat of southern Georgia. It had a tin roof and floorboards that creaked and groaned whenever you walked over them. A swamp ran along one side of the property, and a stream that my father dammed up to create a pond, eventually attracting hundreds of waterfowl. Our home may have been primitive by most standards, but to me it was heaven. I was a little naturalist, spending practically all my time in the woods.

Sylvania was tiny, with a population of about 3,000 people, and truly rural. I kept myself busy with choir, saxophone, Boy Scouts, and 4-H. By high school, we had moved to a new farm. This one was larger—a little over 500 acres—with ponds and sprawling pine forests. I was certainly less interested in schoolwork than I was in getting home after school to explore the woods, hunt and fish, and just be out in nature. I saw homework as a hindrance, keeping me from the outdoors and the sports I excelled in: swimming, cross-country, and tennis.

I even started a business of my own, raising purebred Yorkshire pigs. I made a fairly significant amount of money—very helpful during my college years—and I also learned what enormous responsibilities farmers have. From time to time my parents would hitch up a trailer and take us to competitions, me with my prize pigs and my brother with his prize cattle. As part of an Eagle Scout project I helped found the nation's first gopher tortoise reserve, which eventually led to the naming of that threatened species as the Georgia state reptile. And I still spent every spare moment I could scouring plowed fields and eroded gullies—anywhere the earth had been disturbed—in search of Native American artifacts.

Like many kids from small towns, my extracurricular activities gave me a taste of the big world out there, and I liked it. I was elected state president of Georgia 4-H. My pig farm had grown to 50 animals, and mornings before school consisted of a 5 a.m. wake-up to feed my pigs and our hunting dogs. On weekends, I deejayed a morning radio show on a little AM country music station, WSYL, that reached just a few hundred people. I managed to get a Naval ROTC scholarship to Vanderbilt University. Maybe because I never stopped talking, my teachers and family encouraged me to become a lawyer. So I packed up my things and left Sylvania behind for Nashville, Tennessee.

ॐ

COLLEGE LIFE OPENED MY eyes. The NROTC scholarship kept me busy every morning for physical training, while my evenings were increasingly full of new friends, Greek life, and socials. My classes were a different matter. I found I hated economics and political science—in fact, all the pre-law courses. I didn't jell with other students in pre-law, and my grades suffered.

On the other hand, I found my electives at Vanderbilt exciting. I took courses in videography, religion and science, and geology. For the first time I met people who made a career of rocks and fossils. In all my years of reading books about dinosaurs and roaming the fields in search of Native American artifacts, I had never really thought about any of that as a possible career. Yet here were graduate students and scientists who studied the things I loved, and they seemed to be having a great time doing it. After a few weekend field trips to roadcuts looking for fossils, I started thinking, "Could I do this?"

Except I had a problem: The Navy had spent a great deal of money and training to make me a naval officer and a lawyer, and I was busy failing.

My academic adviser was Lt. Ron Stites, a naval aviator and the picture of naval officer success. I was terrified as I stood at attention in front of his desk. He held my future in his hands. There I stood in my white midshipman's uniform, probably trembling with fear, and there was my academic transcript in front of him.

"Berger, what do you see here?" he asked. He slid the paper with my grades on it across the desk. I didn't need to look down to see the numerous D's and F's in my core subjects. The A's and B's in my electives didn't help my GPA very much, and the Navy certainly hadn't brought me here to play with rocks and video cameras. Another semester of grades like this, and I would fail the conditions of my scholarship. If I defaulted, I might have to pay back all the time as an enlisted man.

With all this in mind, I muttered something like "A failure."

A flicker of a smile crossed his face as he shook his head gently from side to side. "No, Berger, I don't see a failure," he said. "Your fellow cadets respect and like you. You're a natural leader. It's your grades." He tapped my transcript. "I see someone who hasn't found what he loves to do." He was pointing to my grades in geology. I remember glancing up from this finger to his face, a bit startled and confused. Here was a naval officer and my academic adviser, and that was the last thing I expected him to say.

He watched me for a moment, and then he asked, "What are you going to do about it?"

I gave a small shake of my head, shrugging a bit. I honestly didn't know. My whole life had been planned with just a limited number of options. Bright kids from rural Georgia had three or four pathways: Doctor, lawyer, engineer, maybe accountant—those were the tickets out.

"Maybe I should enlist for a while, find myself?" I said.

He shook his head. "No, you don't belong in the enlisted Navy, Berger." He looked me over for what seemed like an eternity.

"I'll tell you what I will do," he finally said. "If you commit to me that you will deregister from this degree before your grades get any worse, get out of college for a while, and go do something constructive, find what you love, and then come back, I will release you right now from any obligations you have to the Navy."

I was stunned. This was my get out of jail free card, and at least it gave me motivation.

"Yes, sir, thank you, sir," I nodded. And with that, I did just as he suggested.

My reception back home was, to be generous, lukewarm. I was supposed to be this success story—Eagle Scout, state president of 4-H, naval scholarship winner—and yet here I was, back home in Georgia, having all but flunked out of college. My parents were disappointed. But luckily, I had my pig money to support me while I tried to sort out my life.

# 2

I rented an apartment in Savannah and started taking some courses in videography at the Savannah College of Art and Design. I offered to work at a local television station, WSAV, for free, and soon they had me hauling the enormous cameras around, training in teleprompter duties, and within two months, working beside the director, training to run live news. I started envying the life of the field reporters: men and women in their 20s at the forefront of the action. I hatched another plan, and soon I was working full-time as a news photographer.

One thing led to another. I still today consider my time as a cameraman some of the most fun I have ever had. We would sit in the newsroom and monitor the police radio frequencies. Sometimes we raced to a scene, either alone or with a reporter; sometimes we would cover a planned event. For a 20-year-old, it felt like riding a roller coaster. A call would come in at ten o'clock at night, just an hour before the news at 11. The producer would shout, "Get me footage for the headlines!" and I was on my way. I knew the score: This could be the lead story, and whichever station had video would win the night.

Thus began my journey as a night crime news photographer. Paired with a young producer, Beth Hammock, we became a two-person newsroom with the freedom to chase any story. Our shift began at 11:30 in the evening and ended after the morning news at 6:30 a.m. Usually, I would patrol the early parts of the morning in high-crime-rate areas, trying to bump into a story.

Catching up with police officers, many of whom became good friends, and monitoring the police frequencies became my nightly routine. It was exciting, fulfilling, and Beth and I felt like we were pioneers.

I was having a great time, but eventually I had to come to terms with the fact that I was out of my element. My colleagues were all trained professionals. It was time for me to finish college, but I knew this really wasn't the career path for me. So I enrolled at East Georgia State College, a two-year school. I met some remarkable professors there, passionate about geology and history. I learned that ancient marine deposits in southern Georgia might contain dinosaur fossils. One long weekend, I loaded up the back of my canopied Ford Ranger with an inflatable mattress, sleeping bag, and supplies borrowed from my geology professor, and went fossil hunting.

Georgia's geology is defined by the fall line, which cuts through the state roughly southwest to northeast between Columbus and Augusta. The ancient coastline of the Atlantic Ocean, the fall line represents a geological divide between older and younger rock formations. The fall line region itself is underlain by more ancient rocks and has attractive rolling hills of mixed hardwoods and pines. Below the fall line stretches a relatively flat landscape, a coastal plain with sediments ranging in age from the late Cretaceous (65 to 80 million years ago) to only a few thousand years old.

I found a likely spot at a river bend and began sieving. Soon I had collected a wonderful array of well-preserved marine invertebrates: large fossil clams, sharks' teeth, sharks' feces (preserved shark poo), fish and ray remains—even the odd bit of dinosaur bone. This was real treasure hunting. I spent the next three days waking up at dawn and wading into that river, collecting hundreds of fossils from the age of the dinosaurs. My geology professor greeted the discoveries with great enthusiasm. I was hooked on fossil hunting!

One afternoon, doing research for a history report, I found a title in the card catalog: *Lucy: The Beginnings of Humankind*. I pulled the paperback off the shelf and read as Donald Johanson and Maitland Edey described the search for human origins in the Afar region of Ethiopia. I was entranced.

That evening, I left the library not only with *Lucy* but with every other book I could find on the subject of early human fossils. I had been leaning toward studying dinosaurs, thinking about Georgia's fossil beds, but this work fascinated me, even though it could only be done in Africa.

I was astounded to read about how scarce the human fossil record really was. Our distant ancestors weren't like dinosaurs, with thousands upon thousands of remains. The partial skeletons of hominins that had been found could be counted on one hand. Here was a field where I might make a difference, where new exploration and discovery might change science.

I needed to go to a bigger school, and I chose Georgia Southern University. Close to Sylvania, it was still a midsize school, with the small town of States-boro nestled around it. Beyond lay the vast areas of rural Georgia where I had grown up.

My time at Georgia Southern was filled with fieldwork in paleontology and archaeology. I spent every spare hour in the lab, sorting micro-mammal remains from marine sediments, preparing whale bones with a drill, gluing together mosasaur ribs, washing and labeling artifacts, or identifying pottery sherds. My professors were passionate about their work, and they had a profound impact on my life. Gale Bishop, a world-renowned invertebrate paleontologist and perhaps the world's leader in fossil crabs, introduced me to fossil discovery methods. Richard Petkewich, a fossil mammologist, trained me in lab methods and fieldwork in the muddy estuaries around Savannah. I helped him with the prepa-ration of an archaeocete, an ancient legged whale, which had been found near the nuclear power station on the Savannah River. I spent hours with anthropology professors Sue Moore and Richard Persico, discussing the history of my new favorite subject, paleoanthropology.

But was I going to be a dinosaur paleontologist or a paleoanthropologist? And if the latter, how would I ever get to Africa, where the fossils were?

Again, serendipity played a role in my future. Donald Johanson, discoverer of Lucy and my hero of modern paleoanthropology, had been invited to give a lecture to the Georgia Science Teachers Association in Savannah. Here was my chance to meet a real field paleoanthropologist. We hit it off well enough that he invited me to come work as a geology assistant with his team at the Olduvai Gorge in Tanzania. It was my chance to do fieldwork in Africa! But that trip never materialized. I found out later it had to do with work permit issues in Tanzania. Still, thanks to Don Johanson's help, I was accepted into a summer program at the Koobi Fora Field School in Kenya, where the celebrated paleoanthropologist Richard Leakey's famous "hominid gang" was exploring new fossil sites on the east side of Lake Turkana.

That was 1989; I was 24 years old, and Africa turned out to be everything I had dreamed of and more. On my first excursion into the field, as I was just learning how to find fossils in those ancient lake environments, I spotted something lying on the lake's barren surface and pulled up a fragment of thighbone—a piece of a hominin femur. I was hooked!

# 3

On New Year's Day 1990, I arrived in South Africa with the hope of finding hominin fossils. It was an unlikely place for an American student. The nation was still under the rule of the National Party, the apartheid government. Growing up in Georgia in the 1960s, I knew something about the evils of racial discrimination, and had seen firsthand the changes brought by integration. In South Africa, the winds of change were blowing, too. The government released Nelson Mandela from his long imprisonment in February 1990, and the end of apartheid was on the horizon.

I had been accepted as a Ph.D. student at the University of the Witwatersrand. Known to staff and students as "Wits," the university is in the heart of downtown Johannesburg. Wits was semi-independent, but the government held the purse strings for the vast majority of research. Human evolution research could not be a priority, because it challenged the premise of apartheid by showing the common origin of all humankind. By the late 1980s, the science was clearly showing that our evolutionary roots began in Africa. The work of many scientists, in South Africa and elsewhere, defied the racial logic of the National Party. Research showed that there was no "natural" separation of the races—but that didn't mean the apartheid government had to like it.

So paleoanthropology in South Africa was struggling. The science of human origins—a strength of the country for 70 years—was in visible decline. Wits was the university where the science of human evolution in

Africa had gotten its start, and the home institution of Phillip Tobias—a living link to the field's early history for me and many other anthropologists of my generation. A student of the late, great Raymond Dart, considered the father of African paleoanthropology, Phillip Tobias tied 70 years of discoveries together with his work. For me, learning this history was part of learning the field of paleoanthropology.

IN 1922 RAYMOND DART had come to Wits from Australia—then a hinterland of the British Empire, like South Africa—and had become a professor of anatomy. He found an open field with countless questions related to human history and diversity. Archaeologists had started to make some progress understanding the ancient peoples of southern Africa. Dart dived in, examining fragmentary skeletal remains that archaeologists sent to the department. Writing in the internationally respected journal *Nature,* he emphasized that South Africa had its own store of ancient races, just as interesting and ancient as the Neanderthals and Cro-Magnons of Europe.

In 1924 one of Dart's students, Josephine Salmons, showed him a fossil baboon skull found in the Buxton Limeworks, near the town of Taung in what is today South Africa's North West Province. It interested Dart, and he asked the limeworks to send any other rocks with bones. One that came was a natural fossil cast of the inside of a skull, called an endocast, from a large primate. It was exquisite, preserving much of the internal surface of the skull on the right side, its left side encrusted like a geode with sparkling crystals.

But this was no monkey, Dart immediately recognized. The brain was much larger than that of any baboon yet much smaller than any known human ancestor. Could it be a fossil of some kind of ape? It seemed unlikely, because the nearest apes—chimpanzees or gorillas—lived more than a thousand miles away.

Then Dart spied another rock. It contained part of a jawbone that connected with the endocast like a puzzle piece. There was a face inside the rock. For weeks, he removed chips of rock, slowly exposing the face of a tiny child with a full set of baby teeth and its first permanent molars just coming in. As he studied the precious specimen, he became convinced that this was like no ape anyone had ever seen before.

Dart sent his conclusions to *Nature,* which published them in February 1925. This skull was more humanlike than any of the living apes, yet it was not human. He called it a man-ape, and gave it the name *Australopithecus africanus,* meaning "southern ape from Africa."

Charles Darwin had predicted that humans had originated in Africa. Now, with this African fossil much closer to humans than any living ape, Dart could show Darwin's hunch to be right. In a matter of months, with the fossil that came to be known as the Taung Child, Raymond Dart had rewritten the story of human origins.

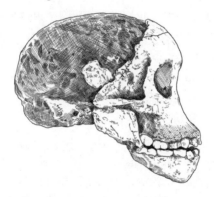

*The skull, jaw, and endocast of the Taung Child*

But a single fossil, extraordinary as it was, left plenty of room for argument. To begin with, it was just a child. Humans resemble juvenile apes more than we resemble adult apes, a fact that argued for caution. Another problem was the Taung Child's posture. Using the broken base of the skull as evidence, Dart suggested that it stood upright. But other experts wanted to see bones of the lower limb—bones that Dart did not have. They also wanted to see the teeth, which Dart had not yet fully cleaned.

Experts looking at such a fossil, even today, consider three basic questions: How big was its brain? Did it stand upright? Are its teeth humanlike? These key characteristics help separate humans from apes: That was evident even to Charles Darwin in 1871, when the only ancient human fossils known were those of the Neanderthals, found in Europe.

Darwin had tied these three key characteristics together into one scenario of human origins: Larger brains made our ancestors more clever, leading them to develop tools and weapons. They needed free hands, and natural selection thus favored upright walking. Carrying new weapons, these ancient ancestors no longer needed large canine teeth. Other evolutionary developments were simply consequences of these three basic changes.

This scenario suggested that over time, our ancestors' brains, posture, and teeth evolved in tandem with each other. The place of any fossil on this line of development should reflect its geological age. The older it is, the more like an ape the fossil would be. Where did the Taung Child fit in?

Raymond Dart had no solid idea how old these fossils might be. Baboon fossils found in similar crevasses within the rock were close to modern species, suggesting that the Taung Child might not be very old—but perhaps that did not contradict the idea that Taung lay between humans and other apes: a missing link in evolution.

Evolution gives rise to a tree of species whose branching formations and relationships paleoanthropologists seek to describe. For Dart, *Australopithecus* represented an unknown branch from the human stem, and one that offered evidence about the earliest period of human evolution. Other paleoanthropologists entered the scene, including Robert Broom, a Scottish physician who had worked for decades on South African fossil species, from reptiles to baboons. As Dart withdrew, wounded by skepticism expressed by colleagues about his discovery, Broom rose to the occasion, determined to find an adult fossil to match the Taung Child.

Students of Dart had been examining an impressive cave called Sterkfontein, about 50 kilometers northwest of Johannesburg, situated beneath a hillside rising up from the little Bloubank River. Visitors today pass through its natural opening and emerge into a yawning cavern with a great slope of loose debris. Huge stalactites and columns are visible, while side passages hide deeper secrets, including deep fossil-bearing chambers and an underground lake. Above the cave today, a catwalk stretches over a jumbled pit the size of a baseball diamond, full of blasted breccia, where scientists still work, finding fossils of hominins and other creatures.

In the 1930s, Sterkfontein was a working lime quarry. Raymond Dart's students had been collecting monkey fossils there, and Broom accompanied them on one of their visits. Picking through the waste breccia piles, he found crushed pieces of face and jaw as well as worn teeth. These fossils were smashed, but they did provide him with evidence of the adult he was looking for, today identified alongside the Taung Child as *Australopithecus africanus.*

Over time, many more hominin specimens surfaced at Sterkfontein, including bones from the rest of the skeleton. Most striking was the skeleton of an adult female, with spine, ribs, pelvis, and parts of the legs, known as Sts 14. These postcranial bones—bones from parts of the body below the skull—revealed that the Sterkfontein species had stood upright and walked like humans.

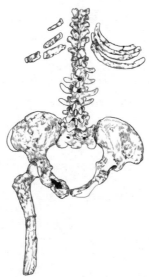

*Skeleton of Sts 14 from Sterkfontein*

Even more exciting, Sterkfontein was not alone. There were caves and breccia deposits all up and down the valley. In 1938 a local boy handed Broom a fossil found on a farm just a kilometer east of Sterkfontein. Exploring the breccia there, Broom and his team recovered part of a hominin skull and a jaw more massive than those from Sterkfontein, with larger molar teeth. Broom recognized it as a different species, now called *Paranthropus robustus.*

Later, working at a cave just to the west of Sterkfontein called Swartkrans, Broom found more massive jaws and molars of *robustus.* Meanwhile, Raymond Dart and his student Phillip Tobias began fieldwork at a site called Makapansgat in the Northern Province, which ultimately yielded more fossils of *Australopithecus africanus,* like those from Sterkfontein.

It was a golden age for paleoanthropology in South Africa. Between 1936 and 1951, the fossil hominin record grew to scores of specimens from five more major sites. Broom published several books with scientific descriptions of the new fossils he had found, and Dart launched a series of new provocative ideas about the way these early human ancestors may have used tools and fire.

Then, discoveries of new early hominin sites stopped.

That is not to say all research stopped. The known sites would continue to be the focus of work for years, continuing up to today. And archaeologists in other parts of the country turned up a few fossils of ancient humans along with much evidence of their tools and the animals they hunted for prey. But no one was finding new fossil sites, at least not in South Africa. For a while, it seemed that all the excitement was in East Africa.

# 4

The paleoanthropology of East Africa goes back to the 1920s, when Louis Leakey started searching for evidence of ancient humans in Kenya and Tanzania. At first with other colleagues and later with his wife, Mary, Louis investigated dozens of sites. They found ancient human skeletal remains, some of the earliest tools, and ape fossils that he believed might be forerunners of *Australopithecus*.

The most promising of their sites was Olduvai Gorge, where the Leakeys worked for many years. There, for countless millennia, sediment had settled in streambeds and lakeshores, scattered with animal bones and stone tools stacked one atop the other like an ancient layer cake, until erosion cut through like a knife, forming the gorge. The deepest part of the site was the oldest, known as Bed I. And in those deep sediments, Mary and Louis had found rudimentary stone tools that they called "Oldowan."

In 1959, Mary found fossil hominin teeth there as well. Working over a few weeks, she and Louis recovered the pieces of a marvelous skull, almost complete. Louis called it Mary's "Dear Boy," and they suspected they had found the maker of their Oldowan tools. By their best reckoning, based upon the extinct animal fossils found at the site, the tools and the skull were a bit more than a half million years old. In a short paper they described their discovery, giving it the name *Zinjanthropus boisei*. The world came to know Mary's "Dear Boy" as "Zinj."

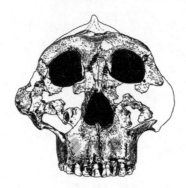

*The "Zinj" skull*

A month after Mary had found the first teeth, the Leakeys brought the skull to Johannesburg to share with Raymond Dart and Phillip Tobias and to compare their find with South African fossils. Zinj had vastly larger molars than *africanus* but many of the same features as *robustus*. As other scientists learned about the Zinj skull, many of them considered it a close-enough match to the South African *robustus* that they rejected the Leakeys' idea that it was a new species. Today most accept *boisei* as a separate species but group it as a close relative of *robustus*.

During the Leakeys' next field season at Olduvai Gorge, they discovered two fragments of skull, a jaw, and part of a hand that clearly came from a creature with a bigger brain yet smaller jaw than Zinj. Later, they unearthed more skull and jaw pieces, all from a similar kind of hominin. The result was plain: Another creature, closer to humans, had lived at Olduvai near the same time as Zinj. Perhaps this species, not Zinj, was the toolmaker.

The Leakeys assigned the new fossils to a new species, which they named *Homo habilis*. The name, which meant "able man," reflected their hypothesis that *habilis* had made the stone tools in Bed I of Olduvai. The idea was that the invention of stone tools had set us on a human path, triggering evolutionary changes toward larger brains and hands that could use tools. The new fossil hand seemed well suited for tool manufacture, including broad fingertips and a long thumb. Yet the *habilis* skulls suggested brains just half the size of those in most people living today.

The most unexpected discovery came in 1961. Physicists at Berkeley had developed new methods for dating ancient volcanic rock. Although these don't occur in the caves of South Africa, many East African sites like Olduvai Gorge do contain ancient layers of volcanic ash. Louis Leakey sent samples from Olduvai, and soon the results came out: The Bed I sites with Zinj and *habilis* were not 600,000 years old, as Louis had assumed. They were 1.75 million years old.

This new date changed the entire outlook of paleoanthropologists. The Olduvai tools and fossils were far older than any other human artifacts or fossils found anywhere in the world. But this was only the beginning. Louis and Mary had found fossils of extinct apes at sites much older than Olduvai. Somewhere in East Africa, there might be layers containing fossils of the original population that gave rise to all the later hominins, the roots of our family tree.

The quest for these earliest hominins became the major scientific story of human origins during the 1970s and early 1980s. American and French teams planned an expedition with Leakey into the Omo Valley of southern Ethiopia; when Louis's health failed, his son Richard led the Kenya contingent. Omo produced many important fossils, including the earliest modern human skeletal remains, almost 200,000 years old, and earlier hominin remains, many more than two million years old. But no one found fossils to rival those at Olduvai Gorge.

Richard Leakey redirected his fieldwork efforts to the shores of Lake Turkana, in northern Kenya's Rift Valley. There, throughout the 1970s and 1980s, he and his wife, Meave, led a skilled team of fossil hunters who became known as the "hominid gang"—the group I was fortunate enough to work with in 1989, during my first summer experience in Africa.

The early discoveries from Lake Turkana included remarkable fossils, including a skull then thought to be the earliest specimen of *Homo* from anywhere in the world. Scientists today identify it as the best example of the species *Homo rudolfensis,* a contemporary of *habilis.* In 1984, the hominid gang's most accomplished fossil hunter, Kamoya Kimeu, found the first pieces of a skeleton that would eventually become the most complete

*Homo erectus* yet discovered. Known as Turkana Boy, it is a young male, aged at approximately 1.5 million years old, with many humanlike body structures but key differences in the brain, skull, and teeth.

Meanwhile, in the early 1970s Donald Johanson, a brash young scientist from the United States, joined a field expedition at a site in Ethiopia called Hadar. The team found hominin fossils, including a partial skeleton soon to become the most famous in the world, nicknamed "Lucy." Geological work dated Lucy and associated fossils back more than three million years.

At the same time, Mary Leakey continued to work in northern Tanzania, where she found hominin jawbones and teeth as old as 3.6 million years. Her team also uncovered many sets of fossil footprints made by a creature walking on two legs. Mary invited Tim White, a young American paleoanthropologist, to work on formal descriptions of the fossils. When White compared notes with Johanson, they developed the idea that the Tanzanian and Ethiopian fossils represented a single species, the earliest hominin then known. They named it *Australopithecus afarensis*.

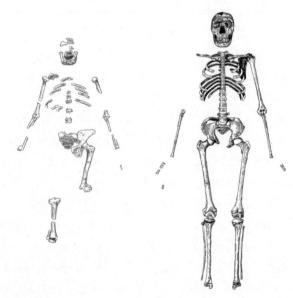

*The skeleton of Lucy (*Australopithecus afarensis, *left), compared with a* Homo erectus *skeleton (right)*

The discoveries of the Leakeys, Don Johanson, and others constituted a second golden age of paleoanthropology. They shaped the science over the succeeding decades. These were the scientists whose work so thrilled me that I eagerly entered their field of study. They remained active during the years that I was a student and young professional, and they contributed profoundly to my own knowledge of human evolution. Their discoveries, and those of other scientists, have continued to expand the fossil record of human origins during the last 25 years, adding many more species to our family tree—some immediately accepted by most scientists in the field, others considered controversial. As I enrolled at Wits to take up paleoanthropology as my career, these scientists were predominant in a field that no longer looked to South Africa but instead looked to East Africa as the important setting for human origins.

# A DEPICTION OF THE FAMILY TREE OF HOMININ SPECIES

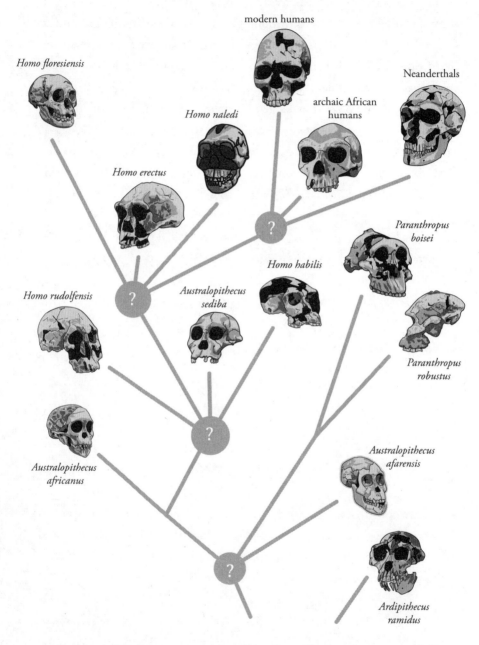

modern humans

*Homo floresiensis*

Neanderthals

*Homo naledi*

archaic African humans

*Homo erectus*

*Paranthropus boisei*

*Homo habilis*

*Homo rudolfensis*

*Australopithecus sediba*

*Paranthropus robustus*

*Australopithecus africanus*

*Australopithecus afarensis*

*Ardipithecus ramidus*

*Building this tree is a continuous effort of new fossil and genetic analyses, and the question marks indicate places where we cannot yet be sure of the order in which to place the branches. Please note: Not every species that has been proposed is included, especially in the lowest branches.*

# 5

Today the fossil record of human evolution can be divided roughly into three parts. Each has its own cast of characters, some species uncovered by paleoanthropologists, some populations revealed by DNA discoveries. The first and oldest of these parts is the most shadowy.

The lineage of humans and our hominin relatives divided from the ancestors of chimpanzees sometime around seven million years ago, a date estimated by comparing the full DNA of humans and other primates. A handful of fossil discoveries represent this earliest time period of our evolution, from 7 million up to around 4.3 million years ago, the most important discovered during the 1990s by the field team of Tim White, the same young researcher Mary Leakey had worked with in Tanzania 20 years before.

The best of these fossils is a partial skeleton found in the Middle Awash region of Ethiopia and given the name *Ardipithecus ramidus*. Its anatomy reveals an ape the size of a male chimpanzee with a brain around the size of a chimpanzee's as well. With opposable first toes, short thumbs, and extremely long fingers, *Ardipithecus* seems to have been as good in the trees as the great apes of the present day. But it had some features more like those of later members of the human lineage: smaller canine teeth, a more compact pelvis, and a skull that seems to have rested atop a vertical spine. *Ardipithecus* did not walk on two legs like humans, but it may have held itself more upright than apes do today.

Beyond that important discovery, fossil fragments have been found from more ancient sites, representing species with names like *Sahelanthropus tchadensis* and *Orrorin tugenensis.* But they preserve only bits of the anatomy, making it hard to know much about them. These species have been found in eastern or central Africa—but so far we have not found any hominin fossils from this early time period in southern Africa.

The second great part of human evolution, between 4.2 million and 1.5 million years ago, is represented by the range of species known as australopiths, including Raymond Dart's *Australopithecus africanus* and Robert Broom's *Paranthropus robustus.* These species all walked upright, as indicated by a pelvis, legs, feet, and spine that share features with the bones of modern humans. They would have been as awkward on all fours as people are today, but they also seem to have retained the ability to climb. Australopith bodies were small compared with humans today, and their brains averaged a third the size of ours. All had big premolar and molar teeth, and some had even larger molars and massive jaw muscles, allowing them to rely on a wide range of foods. They lived across sub-Saharan Africa, but no trace of them has been found on any other continent.

The third part of our evolutionary history began around 1.8 million years ago with the species known as *Homo erectus,* the first hominin to emerge from Africa and spread into other parts of the world. It had a body that was human in size, and a brain about 50 percent larger than the brain of any of the australopiths. Anthropologists believe that this larger body and brain enabled *Homo erectus* to navigate larger territories, use stone tools, and eat a higher-quality diet, including meat obtained by hunting. For many anthropologists, these early populations of *erectus* were truly the first humans.

Over hundreds of thousands of years, *erectus* and its descendants branched into varieties and species living in different parts of the world, including the Neanderthals, all grouped together by paleoarchaeologists in the category of "archaic humans." Africa remained the center of our evolution, home to the greatest diversity of these archaic humans and ultimately the place where modern humans arose.

Great discoveries in genetics during the past 10 years have shown that the later part of our evolutionary process was very complex. Humans today owe the vast majority of our heritage to the first modern human populations in Africa, which lived only 200,000 years ago.

We do not know why, but the African population grew and began to spread again across the rest of the world. When it did, those people came into contact with Neanderthals and other populations. Some members of those different varieties of humans mixed their DNA into the growing modern human gene pool. Eventually these modern humans, still mostly African in heritage, spread throughout the world, migrating to places including the Americas and Australia, where no people before them had ever lived. Some 10,000 years ago, people in the Near East, and later in other parts of the world, developed agriculture, an innovation that contributed to the massive recent growth of the human population.

Science has achieved rapid progress in the third major part of our evolution, making the story at once more complicated and more interesting. But who were the ancestors of these first humans, and what set them on a different path than the australopiths? The australopiths were successful and diverse. They existed for more than two million years before the first species that we describe as humans arose. So far, our tremendous progress in genetics can tell us nothing about these extinct branches of our family tree. We rely upon fossil discoveries for that information.

Those fossil discoveries have been frustratingly fragmentary. At one time almost everyone assumed that *habilis* led to *erectus,* which then led to *sapiens.* This was the textbook version of human evolution, a story of direct descent that is probably familiar to many readers of this book. But as new fragments have been added to the fossil and archaeological records, the picture has become more complicated. Over the years, scientists have revisited the original *habilis* discoveries and now point out that we know almost nothing about their bodies. What little we do know suggests that they were very much like australopiths and not very human-like at all.

In Louis Leakey's time, it had seemed that stone tools had been intimately connected with the evolution of *habilis* and *erectus*—so much that *habilis* was imagined as the original toolmaker. But during the 1990s and 2000s, the record of stone tools was pushed back earlier and earlier. In 2015, evidence of early stone tools was found near Lake Turkana in an ancient layer more than 3.2 million years old, nearly double the age of the Olduvai Gorge discoveries. These tools existed long before any of the fossils we have found of hominins with a large brain, even the brain of *habilis*. A few fossil specimens between three and two million years old have been attributed to *Homo,* the earliest being part of a jaw from Ethiopia. But none of these fossils gives us anything indicating the size of the brain.

In other words, the transition from australopiths to *Homo* still raises some of the most compelling questions in our evolution. We cannot answer those questions without better fossil evidence. Maybe there was something worth discovering in South Africa.

# 6

By 1996, I was well established as a young academic. I was 31 years old. I had been teaching human anatomy to medical students for years. I had found fossil hominins in the field, and I had done some good science on those finds in the laboratory. I had a strong publication record and had found ways to fund and support my work. Promoted to senior research officer and director of paleoanthropology, I became responsible for the precious collection of fossil hominins held in Wits's vault. I thus took over the role and responsibilities Phillip Tobias had held for decades.

A generational shift was happening. Younger scientists were introducing technology and new ways of thinking into our profession. My generation was more collaborative by nature, perhaps driven by our familiarity with computers and the Internet, and I was beginning to explore how to broaden the study of these fossils in our vault and encourage more open access.

Both my more senior colleagues and the university urged caution. On my appointment, the deputy vice chancellor of research called me into his office to give me these words of advice. "Lee," I remember him saying, "you have a good publication record, but you have too many collaborators. What you need are more single-authored papers. Those are all you will ever be judged on." For his generation, great science arose from years of lone research or at the most work in small collaborative teams.

I had other ideas. The fact is, my generation approached science differently. For us, new research depended on specialized technology, and no single person could learn all the methods now available to answer the most interesting questions. We could do better science by working together, sharing information and sharing credit. People could collaborate over vast distances, sometimes without ever meeting in person. The Internet was changing the nature of science, enabling publications to appear faster. At the same time, universities and administrators were expecting higher and higher production. We were on the edge of the "publish or perish" cliff, still judged by individual output, even though our productivity was higher when we collaborated.

Collaboration posed a special problem for young paleoanthropologists. The older generation of fossil discoverers could sometimes feel like an exclusive club, and as the new director in charge of the fossil remains, it was as if I had been given a key to the clubhouse. But I represented a generation that didn't just want the keys to the club; we wanted to open the doors to everyone. We were impatient for a faster pace of discovery and science, and sought collaborations with larger and larger groups of experts outside the traditional schools of thought. My instincts for such open collaboration would lead me into conflict with members of my mentor's generation.

ᘒᖶᘐ

IN THE MEANTIME, I got busy. I worked to describe a series of footprints dated to just under 120,000 years ago, found at a place called Langebaan Lagoon, near Cape Town. I hypothesized that they were the oldest known footprints made by a modern human. I described some fossil hominin remains from Saldanha Bay, north up the coast from Cape Town, that I had uncovered back in 1993. I conducted studies to try to understand how the behavior of animals like leopards and hyenas affected the accumulation of bones in caves. And I kept on excavating and operating field schools at Gladysvale, working with Peter Schmid, from the University of Zurich in Switzerland, and later with my longtime friend, Steve Churchill, from Duke University.

In 1997, the National Geographic Society awarded me its first Research and Exploration Prize, recognizing me for "outstanding contributions to the increase of geographic knowledge through his accomplishments in the field of palaeoanthropology." This award came with a cash prize, which I used as it was intended: for research and exploration. I put together a three-year-long expedition to search for new fossil sites in southern Africa. I called it the Atlas Project. From 1998 through 2000, my small teams scanned satellite images to spot potential fossil sites and then carried handheld GPS units out in our small fleet of Land Rovers to plot their locations on the ground. There was no Google Earth in those days. Eventually, high-quality satellite images would become available to all over the Internet, but in the 1990s they came at a huge cost, both in dollars and in computer processing power.

We had some pretty good successes. Before we started, we knew of only a few fossil-bearing sites across the dolomitic limestone stretching from Pretoria across the northern rim of the Johannesburg metropolitan area. These included the famous fossil sites of Sterkfontein and Swartkrans—14 sites in all, the result of some 60 years of exploration. During the course of the Atlas Project, we scoured what I thought was every inch of this region, walking hundreds of kilometers over the rugged terrain and inspecting outcrops and clusters of trees for fossil or cave sites. By the end of the project, we had found the entrances to nearly 30 previously unknown caves as well as four new fossil sites on the surface.

We also extended our search to other areas of South Africa and to Botswana, thanks to a letter from the president, Festus Mogae, giving us permission to survey his country. Over those three years, we found many dozens of fossil localities, most in deposits from ancient rivers. We published our results, describing the sites and the fauna we had discovered, and opened up excavations at one of those new sites, a place called Motsetse, on the property next to Gladysvale. Motsetse would turn out to be rich in saber-toothed cat fossils. But in these days, another hominin discovery still eluded me.

During these expeditions, I began experimenting with bringing the science live to the public. With National Geographic, I started an online column called "Outpost: Human Origins @ nationalgeographic.com," which followed my team as we hunted for fossils. We broke new ground as a real-time online chronicle of science for the general public—but we were hamstrung by the technology of the day. I transmitted reports over my satellite phone. Easy photo uploads and ubiquitous Internet access were years away. The Outpost experiment was short-lived, but it gave me the bug. I could see the potential of using the Internet to communicate the thrill of exploration. Later, I would come back to this idea of sharing fieldwork as it happened.

Those were some of the best years of my life. I had a wife and two young children, and a successful career in science. I was exploring, and I was responsible for one of the largest collections of hominin fossils in the world. But looming on the horizon was a nasty fight that would leave me scarred, and paleoanthropology in South Africa in tatters. The next few years would almost end my hope of ever building a strong exploration program or making a major discovery.

# 7

The challenges came in two waves: first, professional pressure arising from an influential paper declaring how we all should be conducting paleoanthropology, and next, because of conflicts from within, among my own colleagues at Wits.

By 2000, Tim White was one of the most respected paleoanthropologists in the world. A wiry young scientist from the University of California, Berkeley, Tim had succeeded beyond all expectation in the shark tank of East African paleoanthropology in the 1970s and 1980s. He first worked with Mary Leakey to describe the fossil remains from Laetoli, Tanzania. Later he helped Don Johanson to define those same fossils together with Don's new discoveries from Hadar, Ethiopia, as a new species, *Australopithecus afarensis*. When the Ethiopian government reopened research by foreign scientists in 1989, he returned to make several new discoveries of his own.

As the year 2000 approached, the *American Journal of Physical Anthropology*, one of the premier academic journals in our field, asked prominent scientists to reflect on the discipline at the start of the new millennium. In Tim White's "view on the science," he contrasted scientists and "careerists," suggesting that those who broadcast the excitement of their findings with the general public were somehow less respectable members of the profession, more interested in "paleoanthropological media hype." He invoked a "tragedy of the commons for the profession" in which too many scientists were crowding in to work on too few fossils. Discoveries were on the decline, he predicted: "The best of the African fossil fields have probably already been found and exploited," he wrote. "By harvesting surface fossils from these sites, we are rapidly exhausting them. Their yields have dropped precipitously." He painted a pessimistic picture of the future of paleoanthropology for students and young scholars and seemed to propose the old-style members-only approach as the answer to our problems.

His comments countered much of what I was experiencing. When I read these words in 2000, I was still in the midst of the Atlas Project. We had found scores of new potential fossil sites—not expansive sedimentary exposures like those in East Africa, where rains erode fossil bits out of the soft rock, but limestone caves barely visible from the surface, more like time capsules holding fossils within them. White's commentary hadn't mentioned South Africa at all, likely because at that time, many of the world's leading paleoanthropologists didn't consider South Africa worth mentioning. I felt optimistic: Given what we had already found, I was pretty confident that one of the sites might lead to a significant discovery. Still, even I had to admit that our exploration results had so far been pretty disappointing. In a decade of looking, I had found only a handful of hominin teeth. Seeing these slim results, at the same time such a prominent scientist was going on record that the age of African fossil discovery was ending, I could tell that funding for new exploration in Africa was going to become harder and harder to find.

AT WITS, THESE YEARS represented a slow and often difficult transformation. By 1998 I had settled into my role as director of paleoanthropology, making difficult decisions about the future of the unit. Money remained tight, and it was my job to balance the outflow of money against research results. One of the biggest expenses was the Sterkfontein excavation. Although it had been the most productive site in South Africa, hundreds of fossils sat in the vault, still undescribed. The primary investigator at Sterkfontein was Ron Clarke, and although I respected his work—we had even published a paper together—it looked to me as if research coming out of the cave had dwindled. The huge expense of running the site could not be sustained without productivity, and so I made the decision to scale back at Sterkfontein and let Ron Clarke go.

When Clarke had taken over excavation at the site in 1991, he had inherited many fossils that remained to be properly sorted and identified. In these remains were fossils from an underground chamber, the Silberberg Grotto, which contained some of the oldest fossils from the cave. Among them, Clarke recognized six hominin foot bones, and five of them belonged to a single foot. This exceptional fossil find quickly became known as "Little Foot." Ron Clarke and Phillip Tobias published a paper describing these foot fossils in 1995, arguing that the foot's big toe stuck out quite a bit from the other toes, a shape that might reflect a greater ability to climb than found in living humans.

After that, Clarke continued to investigate the source of that foot. The fossils included a broken-off tibia, or shinbone. He and his field assistants, Stephen Motsumi and Nkwane Molefe, pored over the breccia in the Silberberg Grotto to see if they could find a bone that matched up. Finally they found a fragment stuck in the rock of the grotto with a cross section that matched the tibia. Clarke, Motsumi, and Molefe had been working for months, carefully chiseling away the breccia to expose more of the tibia and ultimately revealing more and more of the skeleton of Little Foot. They uncovered parts of both legs, an arm, and the skull. And there was even more within the rock.

Trouble was, I didn't know about these discoveries when I made the decision to shut down Sterkfontein. For more than a year, Clarke had been working on the most spectacular discovery ever made at the site—a hominin skeleton—and he had been working on it secretly. I saw this skeleton, for the first and last time, in late September 1998. He arranged for me to meet him at the cave, telling me he had something to show me. Phillip and I met him there with the head of the Wits anatomy department, Beverley Kramer. As we entered the small chamber, I was surprised to find a documentary filmmaker there, with a cameraman and sound recorder. Ron had decided to make his discovery public. And there was a skeleton, partially emerging from the rock, an extraordinary discovery by any measure. I was shocked. Why had Ron kept this a secret?

From that moment, things went downhill for me.

A rift had been brewing between Ron and me ever since I had become director back in 1996. Phillip Tobias and I had our own growing differences of opinion as well. I wanted to increase the access we gave to visiting scientists who wanted to come work with our fossil collections. I saw it as a way to maximize the scientific value of the collection and the productivity of the entire unit, but Phillip was growing more and more uncomfortable with that approach. Ron may have been afraid that I would insist on extending access to Little Foot to other researchers, denying him the exclusive credit for his discovery. The tensions between Ron, Phillip, and me would probably have amounted to little, if not for Little Foot. That skeleton became the straw that broke the camel's back.

Little Foot was a discovery of historic proportions, but the situation devastated me. I had been making administrative decisions without the full knowledge of a major discovery right under my nose. Revealed to the public, Little Foot became a press sensation. Repercussions from the conflict rippled through the field. Senior scientists at other institutions weighed in, many of them already irritated by my attempts to open greater access to the Wits hominin fossil collections. Public opinion saw me as a clueless administrator who had wronged the discoverer of the most important fossil find in South African history. After six months of quite vicious exchanges, with no real solution in sight, the university administration decided to divide paleoanthropology into two entities: my own exploration research group and the Sterkfontein research group, led by Ron Clarke and Phillip Tobias. I would have to rebuild my entire program of work, not to mention my reputation within the discipline.

I didn't know it at the time, but this major shake-up had unforeseen benefits, for it forced me to break from the past. The legacy of Dart and Tobias was a vault full of fossils that someone else had discovered. In the long run, my newfound independence from this legacy was liberating. It instilled in me a strong drive to go out and make discoveries of my own. I had the Atlas Project under way, and I could focus my attention on finding something new, not working on old sites and already discovered fossils.

Still, it would take more than eight years under the most trying of circumstances before my independence and persistence paid off.

# 8

In 2003, a small skeleton was discovered by a team of Indonesian and Australian archaeologists on the island of Flores in Indonesia. The find surprised the world when Peter Brown, Michael Morwood, and their co-workers described the skeleton as a new hominin species, *Homo floresiensis*. The skeleton was tiny—barely the size of Lucy's—and it had a tiny brain, only around 420 cubic centimeters. It had other features that resembled *Australopithecus* species, or even apes, but a few aspects of its skull, jaw, and teeth seemed like a shrunken *Homo erectus*. It seemed to be some kind of very primitive hominin, yet the skeleton came from archaeological deposits within a large cave, known as Liang Bua, that were then thought to be only 18,000 years old. Modern humans had been in the area long before that. We know that they settled Australia sometime before 40,000 years ago. Could this have been a tiny island population—survivors from the dawn of hominins—who had met our own species?

The press called them the "hobbits"—and they were a sensation. They dominated the headlines. And when there are sensational headlines in paleo-anthropology, I had come to learn the hard way, there is usually a big fight.

The discovery immediately generated controversy. The discovery team proposed that *Homo floresiensis* was a dwarf population of hominins. The island of Flores itself had always been isolated from the Asian mainland and had its own strange retinue of fossil creatures, including pygmy elephant relatives called stegodons and gigantic lizards, even larger than today's Komodo dragons. The cave had more fragments of skeletons of small hominin individuals and evidence of stone tools, even fire. The team claimed that the tools made by these small-brained hominins had been surprisingly "advanced." Maybe, they suggested, brain size wasn't as important to human evolution as we had thought.

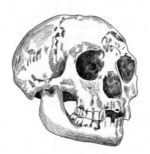

*The skull of the Flores skeleton*

These claims were too much for some scientists to believe, and they went on the attack. Some argued that because modern humans were clearly in the area long before, the Flores skeleton must, in fact, be a form of modern human—probably an individual with some kind of developmental abnormality that affected its body and brain size. Others argued that such long isolation of a hominin population was improbable, especially if they had boats or rafts to reach the island in the first place. Still others doubted that tiny-brained hominins could have mastered stone tools, hunting, and fire.

As this debate heated up, a bitter struggle unfolded for control over the fossil remains. Outside scientists, including some well-established paleo-anthropologists, clamored to study the skeleton and raced to get themselves and their students involved in research on the new find. Others argued that the results of such surprising scientific research should be subject to independent examination. A senior Indonesian scientist, Teuku Jacob, asserted authority over the hominin remains and brought them to his laboratory in Yogyakarta for study, where several other scientists examined them. One member of the original discovery team described this move as a "kidnapping" and, when the bones were returned, decried the damage done to them during their absence.

I could see how the rift over access to fossil specimens was tearing the field apart. Scientists in the powerful and rich countries of the United States, Europe, and Australia were competing with each other for exclusive access to fossil discoveries in poorer countries. They were, in my opinion, using their financial resources and reputations to keep the work for themselves—and dividing the scientific community in the process. It was a problem I recognized well from my experience of trying to open access to the South African fossils. Only a couple of years before the Flores discovery, the 2002 meeting of the American Association of Physical Anthropologists had been the scene of a public dispute about scientific access to fossils. As later reported in *Science* magazine, some scientists came forward with a proposal to establish a database in which scans of fossil specimens would be available freely to scientists. Many paleoanthropologists objected to the idea, arguing that no scans could ever substitute for the original fossils, and that access to the originals should be limited to the discoverers for as long as necessary to fully publish every aspect of their anatomy, a time that might stretch to decades. I spoke in favor of a greater degree of access and collaboration, and later wrote up my views for the association newsletter. What was obvious to everyone was that more was at stake than scientific findings. Researchers wanted to carve out "rights" to exclusivity over fossil discoveries, and they would fight hard to make sure that potential competitors were kept out. In this environment, the idea of open collaboration was a pipe dream.

And then, by accident, I became ensnared in the Flores debate myself.

It began when my wife, Jackie, decided that we needed a family vacation. Over the years, she had learned what to expect from me on a vacation: I would find some way to drag her and our two kids fossil hunting and then end up giving lectures to hotel owners and other guests. This time, she decided to take matters into her own hands, choosing a destination where a fossil site was definitely not in the cards.

Palau is a remarkable island chain perched on the western Pacific Rim. Part of the Federated States of Micronesia, it is made up of hundreds of small and large atolls with crystal clear waters. And these atolls formed recently, so no chance of fossils! We spent the days exploring the islands and beaches, diving and snorkeling. On our second-to-last day, Jackie decided to treat me. She had found an ad in a pamphlet for a kayaking tour that included going into a cave that had "old bones." She was told, on inquiry, that the "old bones" were almost certainly from World War II—and she knew I was a war history buff—so she booked it. The next morning, we spent several hours kayaking among the islands with the children, being shown about by a local guide. A few hours into the tour, we arrived at a small island and were taken into a limestone cave to be shown the "old bones." Indeed, they were old bones, and they were human—I could tell that immediately. In the dim light of the guide's flashlight, I crouched down next to the remains—there was a calvaria, or skullcap, some bone fragments of arms or legs, and broken ribs. They were clearly human, but what struck me immediately was how small they were.

With the Flores debate fresh in my mind, the small skeletal remains posed an interesting problem. The Palauans were modern humans who had reached a remote island some 3,000 years ago. If an ancient hominin like *Homo erectus* could evolve into a small, unusual population on an island, maybe some similar evolutionary processes could affect modern human populations on islands, too. This idea, called "island dwarfing," was already believed to be true of other mammals on islands, but some anthropologists had suggested that culture helped humans deal with the limited resources that might force adaptations in other animal populations. Here, I thought, might be a test case, and it might in the long run shed light on *Homo floresiensis.*

A few weeks later, I found myself in front of a small group of National Geographic staff, showing them pictures and explaining the scientific interest of island dwarfing at this particular time in history. I had already contacted the Palauan authorities for permits to collect some of the remains. We discussed a budget for taking a small group of scientists to Palau, but to make it work, we had to tag on a film crew to support the expedition. So within just a few months of our family vacation in Palau, I was putting together a team of scientists and booking flights for a June 2006 expedition. Jackie simply shook her head in disbelief.

The Palau expedition began with a personal tragedy. In the Philippines, overnighting on the way to Palau from Johannesburg, I received news that my father had been hospitalized. From halfway across the world I had to make one of the most difficult decisions of my life. He had broken his neck in an accident, and his condition was declining. He had been put on a ventilator and would be a quadriplegic for the rest of his life. My father and I were close, and we had talked about just such a situation. He had made it clear that if anything like this should happen, he would want me to continue with the expedition. He had also made his wishes clear about requiring a ventilator for life support. After speaking to my father and then the doctors, I sat alone in my hotel in the Philippines and cried. It is still hard to think about that moment. As my father was transferred to hospice, I continued to the remote island in the western Pacific. A few days later, 9,000 miles away, my father died.

I threw myself into the work at hand. On arrival, we met with tribal elders, presented our goals, and received their blessings. Then, working with the government's archaeological survey, we began work in two caves, the one I had seen and a second we were shown. We learned that these bone-filled caves were actually burial chambers of a sort. Some of the first settlers of Palau, seafaring Polynesians who reached the island some 3,000 years ago, had used certain large caves on the island to place their dead. Over many years, thousands of human remains built up, leaving cave floors literally made of bone fragments. When storms or, occasionally, tsunamis washed into the caves, they scattered and mixed the skeletons together. Some of the original mineral content of the bones was replaced by lime leaching from the bedrock, leaving a thin white coating on many of the bones, including some spectacularly preserved skulls.

The expedition went off as planned, recovering remains from very small-bodied individuals. My longtime friend and colleague Steve Churchill joined me from Duke University on the expedition. Together with researchers and students from Wits, and our Palauan colleagues, we set up a makeshift lab to examine the remains. We started noticing details that seemed unusual.

We found, for example, that the teeth of these ancient Palauans had abnormalities—not surprising for a small population on an island. Similar anomalies had been found on the Flores skeleton, such as premolar teeth out of line. Many of these Palauan skulls had a very slight chin, not a prominent one sticking forward from their jaw. Again, this seemed similar—but not identical—to the Flores skeleton. We began to wonder if, in fact, some of the traits that had been used to describe *Homo floresiensis* were actually just a result of inbreeding and small body size, similar to what we were finding in the bones from Palau. Such features didn't challenge the idea that the Flores population was really a distinct species—we had no opinion about that. But they might show evidence about the process of evolution, and they might suggest that the Flores species should be redefined.

As we prepared our research for publication, we decided to try a relatively new journal, *PLOS ONE,* one of the pioneers in the new wave of open access to scholarly publications. My co-authors and I were, of course, in favor of this trend. Traditional scientific journals had operated by subscription to libraries, but with the advent of the Internet, they had moved toward not only huge subscription charges to libraries but also paywalls that charged for access by individuals. Huge amounts of money were changing hands, but the results of research were not accessible to the public. During the review and eventual publication of this paper in 2008, I first met John Hawks, a young paleoanthropologist and collaborator on this book you are reading.

Meanwhile, though, trouble awaited. As we worked on Palau, the documentary crew followed our every move. Documentary productions maintain their own editorial control—scientists may cooperate with them, but they film, write, and edit the stories. Sometimes that leads to conflict, and it is not uncommon to hear scientists complain about the way that a production has treated their work. In our case, the documentary producers decided that the Flores angle would guide their story. From my point of view, that was a small aspect of the work—it had merely interested me in the broader evolutionary questions. From theirs, it was juicy, complete with a large cast of scientists ready for an argument. As they interviewed experts, word spread that our team was taking a side in the great Flores debate.

We had stumbled onto a battlefield with guns blazing all around us. The prestigious journal *Nature,* which had published most of the original research on *Homo floresiensis,* put a reporter on the story, sending him all the way to Palau. Along the way, he found plenty of critics willing to attack us, almost always for notions that our scientific paper had not proposed.

It would be an uphill fight, getting colleagues actually to read what we had written. They were all too ready to assume that what they read in the media, or saw in a documentary film, must be the accurate scientific story. I learned an important lesson. Scientific debates may, in the long run, be decided by careful scientific work, but in the short run, many scientists pay more attention to the media and the rumor mill. Scientists are smart people, but too often they assume that people who disagree with them must be crackpots or lunatics. It can be the hardest thing in science to look back carefully at your own assumptions and evidence to find why people might disagree.

The scientific debate over the hobbits slowly subsided. Since that time, more information about the Flores fossils has been published, not only by the original discovery team but also by a broader team of paleoanthropologists who became involved in the work. Early archaeological remains, some dating to more than a million years ago, have been found in other parts of the island, and a piece of a tiny jawbone from approximately 700,000 years ago from one of these early sites was first described in 2016. Another tiny brain has not turned up, but research has shown that many features of the skeleton were, in fact, very different from modern humans, and nearly all of them primitive. Probably most important, further archaeological work showed that the initial time line had been wrong. The hominin remains all predated modern humans' arrival. Not everyone is convinced, and there are still many open questions, but in this case, as in all others, scientific progress ultimately depends on reexamining old assumptions, collecting new data, and being willing to put treasured ideas to the test.

The Palau episode hurt as it unfolded, but it would serve me well a few years later, when I had new research on other important finds. I learned to anticipate the problems that media can bring to scientific research, and I found ways to collaborate more constructively with documentary filmmakers. I learned the value of reaching out from the very beginning to a broad range of scientists not involved in the research, to prevent misunderstandings that might cause problems later. I vowed that with my next discovery, if and when I made one, I would take every precaution to prevent such misunderstandings from ever happening again.

I could not know, in early 2008, that just such a discovery was only a few months away.

*Just outside Johannesburg, South Africa, the Cradle of Humankind,
a UNESCO World Heritage site, contains numerous
early hominin sites including Malapa, above, where the fossils
of* Australopithecus sediba *were discovered.*

*Lee Berger's son, Matthew, then nine years old, spotted the first fossil embedded in a block of breccia, or composite rock material, at the Malapa site. "Dad, I found a fossil!" he called out, the first step in a remarkable discovery.*

*The fossil Matthew Berger found at Malapa, a small white intrusion in the breccia rock, turned out to be the clavicle, or shoulder bone, of an ancient hominin.*

*Lee Berger and his son, Matthew, together with their Rhodesian ridgeback, Tau, survey the landscape in which they found fossils of* Australopithecus sediba *in 2008.*

*At Malapa, a pit several meters deep is all that remains
of the ancient cave where fossils formed. Blocks of breccia that included
pieces of two skeletons were blasted out, and the rest of the skeletons
were found in their original locations, indicated here.*

*With Matthew Berger as he made the first discovery
were Job Kibii, at left, a postdoctoral researcher in paleoanthropology
at the University of the Witwatersrand, and Lee Berger,
Matthew's dad—here proudly smiling from the Malapa site.*

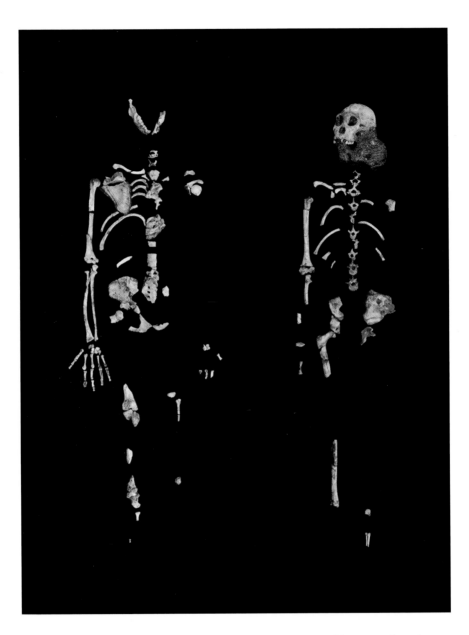

*As the Malapa finds were pieced together, Berger and his team found that they had the better part of two complete skeletons representing* Australopithecus sediba, *an adult female, at left, labeled MH2 (for "Malapa Hominid 2"), and a child, MH1.*

*Particularly remarkable among the Malapa finds was the skull of MH1.
Rarely do researchers come upon an intact early hominin skull,
and this one became a crucial key to understanding the new species.*

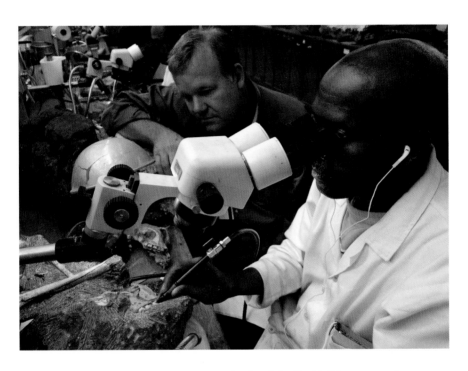

*First viewed via a CT scan, the fossil skull of MH1 required delicate work to extract it from the surrounding rock. Here Lee Berger watches as preparator Pepson Makanela uses an air scribe, a precise compressed air tool, to clean around the teeth.*

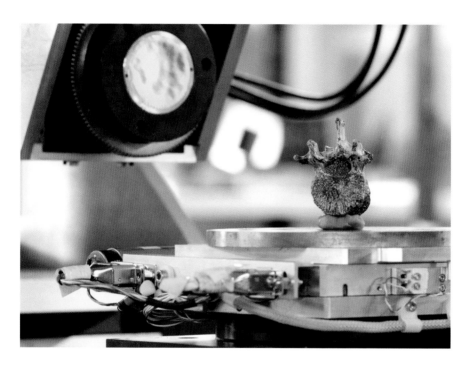

*High-tech meets prehistory: A vertebra from Malapa is set up for scanning to examine its internal details. One of the Malapa vertebrae has yielded the earliest evidence of a benign tumor in the hominin fossil record.*

*Using synchrotron radiation, an advanced type of x-ray analysis, researchers have been exploring the nature of the MH1 skull without damaging it.*

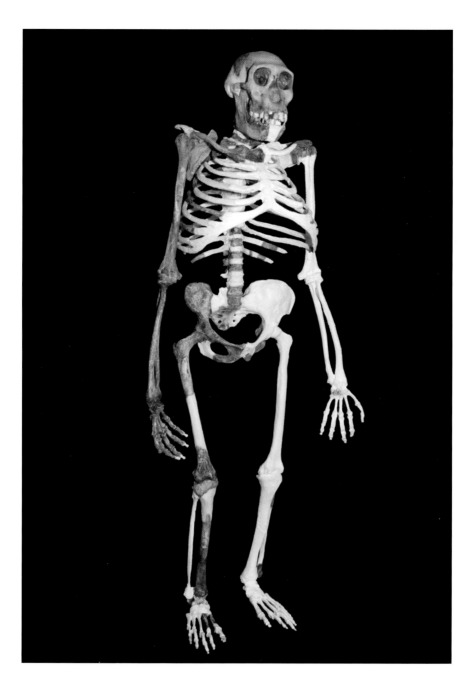

*Basing it on the fossils found at Malapa, Peter Schmid of the University of Zurich, Switzerland, prepared this reconstruction of the* Australopithecus sediba *skeleton. The brown sections reflect the fossil bones actually found.*

*This artist's interpretation illustrates the relative sizes and proportions of three key hominins, left to right:* Lucy *(Australopithecus afarensis),* Malapa's Australopithecus sediba, *and the Turkana Boy (Homo erectus).*

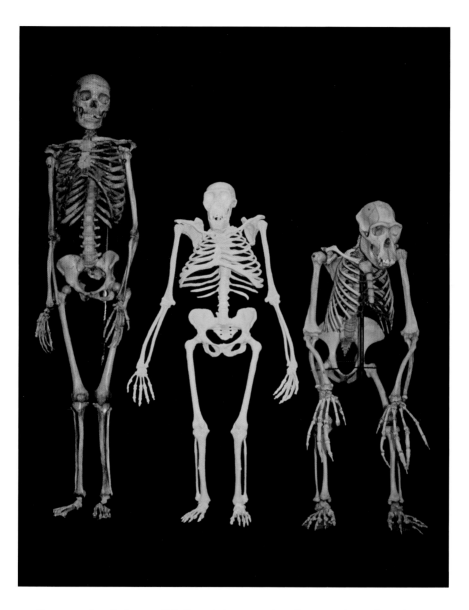

*Comparative skeletons of, left to right, a modern human,* Australopithecus sediba, *and a modern chimpanzee show that although* A. sediba *walked upright like humans, it also shared many features with modern and ancient apes.*

*Thoroughly extracted from the rock that contained it, the skull of MH1 allows us to look right into the face of* Australopithecus sediba.

*Beginning with the excavated skull and building up musculature and soft tissue around it, artist John Gurche reconstructed this life model of* A. sediba.

*How did the bones end up underground at Malapa? One explanation may be that the site represented a prehistoric death trap into which individuals fell and from which they could not escape, as portrayed in this artist's interpretation.*

# PART II
# Finding *sediba*

# 9

"Dad, I found a fossil!" It took me a few moments to recover from the shock of Matt's discovery.

I had a tiny bit of cell phone reception—amazing for our remote location in the middle of the Cradle of Humankind—and I called the national representative of the South African Heritage Resources Agency. SAHRA protects fossil sites and manages permits for excavation. Despite poor reception, I managed to inform the permitting officer of the discovery, who gave me permission to take the fossil from the field. More than one paleoanthropologist has lost a fossil hominin to the elements by leaving it in the field, and we wanted to ensure this one was safe.

Back in my Jeep, Matthew turned to me as he sat in the passenger seat next to me and asked, "Daddy, were you angry at me for finding the fossil?"

I laughed. "Of course not, son—I am more thrilled about it than anything in my life! Why would you think I was angry?"

"Because you cursed when I showed it to you," he said, in all seriousness.

I decided in the future, hominin discovery notwithstanding, I would have to watch my language.

Back at Wits, I filled out the permit application and called the landowners, setting up a meeting to show them the fossil. Enthusiastic about the find, they agreed to give their permission for the permit process.

I sat back and looked at the rock. It was orange-brown in color, with the outline of a mandible, or jawbone, clearly visible, its canine tooth prominently sticking out. The tooth was pearl white, in beautiful condition. Its tip showed little sign of wear, indicating it was from a young individual who hadn't spent years grinding the tooth down on a diet of wild foods. I could see other bones from the outside of the block, every one fairly easy to identify. The clavicle, or collarbone, sat in a horizontal position, about 10 centimeters long and orange in color. And there was the cross section of an ulna—forearm bone—and, near it, a rib fragment, both hominin. Maybe the whole shoulder girdle was inside this block?

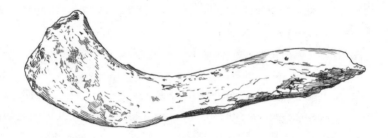

*The piece of clavicle that Matthew first noticed in the rock*

But what species was this? I turned my attention back to the canine—out of all I could see, it was probably the most useful in answering that question. The tooth looked small, and the crown was simple—not the large, sail-shaped canine teeth from Sterkfontein that belonged to *Australopithecus africanus*. And it definitely didn't look like the canine of a robust australopithecine. They tended to be still smaller than this one, with a squat shape.

I shook my head. All of these questions would have to wait for the fossils to be slowly prepared out of this block. That gave some chance of revealing more diagnostic parts, like premolars and molars, and perhaps parts of the cranium itself—the telltale part of the skull that cradled the brain.

Fossils embedded in hard breccia rock material are extracted only with immense skill and care. The process is called "preparation," because the ideal is to prepare the fossil for study. Sometimes conserving the fossil is actually best accomplished by leaving some of the rock, not extracting the whole thing. For their work, the preparators use an "air scribe," a metal device about the size of a large fountain pen, attached to a compressed air hose. The business end of the scribe is tungsten-tipped metal with a sharp, pencil-like point. As compressed air is injected into the scribe, the whole tip vibrates rapidly up and down, a few microns at each pulse. It is as if an ant had invented a jackhammer, throwing tiny shock waves down into the brittle breccia and chipping minute bits of rock away from the fossil bone. Technicians carry out the work under binocular microscopes, their extensive training guiding them as they regulate the speed of the vibration and bring the tip within microns of a fossil, never touching the fossil itself. It often takes more than two years of training on less precious fossils before a technician is ready to work on hominin material.

Preparation is not for the fainthearted. It takes tremendous patience, as a fossil may require thousands of hours of work to be revealed from the rock. It also takes a tolerance of the buzzing noise the scribe makes. The prep room at Wits, with many preparators working at once, sounds like inside a swarm of giant bees. Most find it grating. I, for one, love the noise, because to me it's the sound of discovery.

I went to talk with Charlton Dube, a fossil preparator who worked for the Bernard Price Institute for Palaeontological Research (now called the Evolutionary Studies Institute). He was willing to work on the preparation of this hominin fossil, but he would have to work after hours. My available budget was meager, but I knew I could scrape together enough to pay for the overtime. We agreed on a strategy, starting with the mandible fragment and working around that area, and I left the block with him. Now to await the slow reveal—and the excavation permit.

A few days later I went over to Charlton's prep station to see what he had uncovered. His work nearly took my breath away. There, emerging from the rock, was a beautiful mandible and several molars. Confirming the promise of this rock, the emerging jaw showed there should be other fossils within.

☙

Two weeks later, permit in hand, I was back on the old lime miners' trackway heading up to the site. For now, the site would be known by its number in the Wits system—U.W. 88, the 88th fossil site in our collections. I had put together the trip on the spur of the moment with Job, our postdoc, and more than a dozen people came up the hill behind us.

I smiled to myself, knowing why the trip had attracted such a large retinue. Almost never does a paleoanthropologist have a chance to find a fossil in the wild, so to speak. Now, we were walking up to a place where a nine-year-old had found a hominin fossil in under a minute and a half. How hard could it be? The mood was buoyant.

The old lime miners' track was barely visible, overgrown by grass that was tall and dry in this late winter. As we walked, we were in the direct early morning sunlight, but the path curved up into the shade of a little patch of wild olive and white stinkwood trees. There, just to the right of the path, was a hole in the ground, maybe 10 feet deep and 15 feet across. The sides of this little pit were vertical in places, and we could see that the rock walls were mostly covered with a dark brown mix of soil and breccia. The trees clustered right around the pit. As one walked away, either uphill or down, the ground became a jagged surface of solid stone, foot-wide fingers of bedrock separated by ankle-deep fissures full of grass and brush. A few little animal trails snaked through the landscape. The old miners' track was the one easy route to walk. Twenty meters or so downhill from the pit, across the miners' track, was the lightning-struck tree where Matt had found the hominin block.

Our party scattered, turning over every loose rock, clambering down into the pit, intensely searching the area. Yet we found nothing definitive. We found fossils, but every fragment was hard to identify. Teeth would have been a sure giveaway, but we didn't find a single one. There were no clear postcranial bones of hominins—nothing, that is, from any part of a body below the head. It looked like U.W. 88, like all the other sites in the region, was just full of antelope fossils. The nine-year-old's discovery was looking less like luck and more like magic.

Around 10 in the morning, everyone stopped searching and sat down under a large white stinkwood tree for tea. I didn't join in, frustrated with our lack of success. What if that block Matt found didn't come from this pit at all? I wondered to myself. Matthew had found it 20 meters off the site, quite a distance. Maybe it came from one of the other caves up the hill and had fallen off a miners' wagon as it passed by.

I walked over to the small pit, putting myself on the opposite side of the hole from where Matt had found the first fossil. How had that block gotten there, way across by the lightning-struck tree? From that pit in front of me, I tried to imagine the scene a hundred years ago or more as a tremendous blast of dynamite threw rock and rubble into the air. I imagined miners dropping down into the pit, filled with rubble, tossing rock out into small piles. There the rocks were, still around the pit where miners had thrown them. For the first time that morning, sunlight penetrated the branches overhead, and my eyes traced the back wall of the pit illuminated in the soft winter light. And then I realized it: I was staring straight at the head of a hominin humerus—the upper arm bone of an ancient ancestor.

I blinked in disbelief. I squinted to see better. But the circular head of a hominin humerus was unmistakable. I'd done my Ph.D. dissertation on the hominin shoulder—I knew that shape. We'd already searched that back wall several times that morning. But my eyes were not lying.

I said nothing.

I carefully climbed down into the pit, keeping my eyes on that spot. As I reached the bottom, hearing conversations going on above me, I kept my attention on that bone. Getting closer, the picture became clearer: the head of a hominin humerus sticking perfectly out of the rock! A thin layer of lichen and moss covered it. And there, just below it, cut in cross section, clear as day, was the head and a long, thin section of the scapula—a shoulder blade! It must be an arm of the skeleton Matthew had found—an entire shoulder girdle.

I put my hand out to steady myself against the wall, a few centimeters to the right of the humerus and scapula. I could feel that this part of the wall was actually soft, just dirt. The lichen and moss had probably worked the calcium out of the breccia. As I put weight on my hand, two small rocks dislodged and trickled into my hand. But glancing into my palm, I realized that they were not rocks; they were teeth! Two hominin teeth had just fallen into my hand!

Nothing was keeping me quiet after that.

People crowded around. "Be careful!" I yelled. "They are falling out of the wall and we could be standing on them!" Everyone peered in disbelief at the humerus head, the scapula, and the two teeth I held in my hand.

As I said this, Luca Pollarolo, an Italian archaeologist from Wits, leaned over to pick up a loose rock at my feet.

"Stop!" I shouted, taking him by surprise.

I had seen something on the back of the rock as Luca tilted it upward. It was a hominin femur, clearly a thighbone from a juvenile because its two parts had not yet completely fused into one, indicating it was still growing when this individual died.

What a turn of fortune. Surely this had to be the skeleton of the child whose jaw Matthew had found two weeks before. There it was, I thought, a hominin skeleton in situ—in the exact place in the site where it must have lain for countless centuries.

Four more weeks would go by before I would realize my mistake.

# 10

By early October 2008, I had begun to amass quite the collection of fossils as Matthew's child skeleton—as I had come to think of it—continued to grow. My research group was now so small that I didn't even have a lab anymore, so half of my office became a makeshift hominin laboratory. I covered a heavy circular oak table in velvet, to cushion the fragile fossils, and it became my workbench. I moved a small safe into the corner of the room to hold the fossils and protect them at night.

I named the U.W. 88 site Malapa—"my home" in the southern African language of Sesotho. A fitting name, I thought, not only because Sesotho is widely spoken in the region but also because it is the second language, after English, of Wits University. I made plans for the excavation, deciding where to put a survey beacon so that we could map the site and contextualize the finds. Soon we were ready to excavate the Malapa fossils.

First, there were the blocks on the ground that had been displaced by the miners. We had to map and transport them to the makeshift lab. We plotted the position of the large block with the humerus and scapula and then pried it loose from the wall, lifting it from the pit using sheer muscle and then transporting it back to the lab for preparation.

Each morning, I visited the fossil prep lab to see what had emerged the previous evening. I was now employing five of the Bernard Price Institute preparators after hours, and the growing hominin skeleton had the staff of both institutes abuzz. Day by day, it was exciting to see the fossils emerge.

Bone by bone, the small skeleton took shape as each new piece was added.

First, the mandible was completely prepared out, followed by the small fragment of chin and canine. Then came parts of the upper limb, and some vertebrae were discovered. Eventually, the preparators found half the pelvis, its low, broad shape showing that, indeed, like other hominins, this was a biped. The femur, found on that day in September, began the building of the lower leg. Toe bones and rib fragments followed. After a while, the little skeleton was becoming as close to complete as the famous Lucy skeleton, although without any parts of the skull besides the jawbone. Despite this absence of a head, it was a beautiful thing to behold.

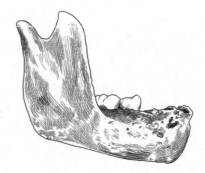

*The first jawbone recovered from the Malapa site, after preparation*

Next Charlton started on the large block containing the humerus and scapula. A day of preparation revealed my mistake in thinking that these parts belonged to Matthew's skeleton: The bones of little children originally form as several parts, connected to each other by thin plates of cartilage. When the bone reaches adult size, the growth plates finally fuse. Hence, a bone that has completely fused, like the humerus that I was seeing in this block of breccia, must have come from an adult. I had already known another individual must be there—the two teeth that had fallen into my hand were from an adult. Now we were finding other adult bones here as well.

To be fair, expecting a second skeleton from this tiny site seemed preposterous. In the entire history of paleoanthropology in Africa, never before had two skeletons been found together in close proximity. There had been assemblages of bones from several individuals found together at a handful of Rift Valley sites and in southern Africa—the most famous probably AL 333, the "First Family" from Hadar, which had fragments of bone from many individuals of Lucy's species, *Australopithecus afarensis*. But nowhere had two nearly complete skeletons been found, right together, in such a small site.

Here, it was definitive: Malapa held two skeletons, both growing before our eyes. As Charlton continued to prepare the block, it became clear that this second skeleton was in fantastic condition. An entire articulated arm began to emerge from the rock. Could there be a hand at the end of the arm? We would have to wait and see.

As I sat in my office, looking at that skeleton laid out on my desk the very next day, I pondered the way forward. How was I going to do this work? I obviously couldn't proceed alone. The science was too specialized, and there was so much to do. It would take a team of experts to understand these skeletons and the site where we had found them.

I thought about the history of discoveries of such skeletons. During the 1970s and 1980s, the teams who discovered fossils tended to publish their first research in a matter of months. The famous Lucy skeleton was discovered in November 1974, and 16 months later, Donald Johanson and Maurice Taieb had published a short description of it. Richard Leakey's team had discovered their most complete find, the famous "Turkana Boy" skeleton, in 1984 and published a first description of the find the very next year. There had been much more research to do on these fossils, which continued for years afterward, but the early tradition had been to carry out the basic scientific description of such discoveries quickly. After all, back in the very beginning of African paleoanthropology, Raymond Dart had published his description of the Taung Child only months after he freed its face from the rock.

But now, in the early 2000s, a new model of how to do science had taken hold. Instead of publishing finds quickly, some of the biggest players in paleoanthropology had been keeping their discoveries close to the vest for many years. Everyone in the field knew that Tim White and his small research team had discovered a partial skeleton of the early fossil species *Ardipithecus ramidus* in the mid-1990s, but since then, White had shared nothing in public about the skeleton's anatomy other than a few cryptic comments. (That team would eventually publish their research on the anatomy of the skeleton in 2009.) Little Foot research was following the same slow release schedule as "Ardi," it seemed, as well. Little Foot had been discovered at Sterkfontein in 1997, and now, nearly a dozen years later, no one outside that group really knew what progress had been made. These discoveries had been extremely challenging for their teams to preserve and prepare. Each team had certainly wanted to do the best possible work on them. Maybe years of study in relative secrecy were really necessary for them to understand and carefully describe what they had found. That was impossible for me to know. What was obvious was that these more recent examples were not alone; other research teams had adopted similar practices.

Malapa, too, would be challenging to prepare, every piece requiring dozens of hours of work. It would surely take years to fully understand the site and recover all the hominin material that must be there. Would it be better to wait until I had a whole skeleton, or even both of them, before publishing? Almost every day, something new was coming out of the rock, and it didn't look like it was going to stop.

Back in 2003, when I had written so strongly in defense of opening access to the South African fossil hominins, I had suffered for it. My strongest critics said that I was "giving away" the hard-won discoveries made by others. That certainly wasn't true about the discoveries from Malapa. Looking at the fossils, thinking about the hours of work each one represented, I knew I had to go with my instincts. I could not keep them closed off from other scientists for years.

Nor could I do it alone. I needed a team.

PAUL DIRKS AND I had collaborated well during the years I had been exploring the Cradle, and I wanted him to lead the geological work. Steve Churchill had been working with me on projects since we had met while both of us were finishing our Ph.D. research. We had recently worked together on the Palau expedition, co-writing the descriptions of that skeletal material. One of the world's leading experts on the postcranial skeleton—the bones of the body beneath the skull—Steve was the logical choice to lead that part of the work. I also knew I wanted Darryl de Ruiter to be involved. Darryl had come to South Africa from Canada in the mid-1990s, first as an undergraduate volunteer and then as a Ph.D. student of mine. In the past several years he had worked extensively on the skulls and teeth of South African hominins. I trusted Darryl and knew he would be up to the task of describing this mandible and the two adult teeth.

I sent Steve and Darryl an email on October 11, 2008, pictures attached, entitled simply "Hominids."

Their excited replies came back within hours. Looking at the pictures of the mandible, both of them shared a first impression. It looked like an australopith, maybe even a robust one. I knew that first impressions, and pictures, could be misleading, and I hadn't attached a scale. But their minds had gone to work right away, shaping their first thoughts on how to tackle the problem. It wasn't so bad a guess—so far, in the Cradle, australopiths were exactly what we expected to find. Both of their opinions would change over the next weeks as they examined the pictures sent to them, and they became more and more convinced that the little mandible was something special.

At about this same time, Peter Schmid, another longtime colleague and friend, called from Zurich. Peter and I had run field schools together, and now he wanted to know if I would be interested in another. His students had loved working in South Africa and were interested in a return to Gladysvale.

I interrupted him, "There is something you need to see."

Two weeks later, Peter was in my office, looking skeptically at the table where I had draped a cloth over the little lumps of fossil, hiding the skeleton from view.

Peter is what one would call an "old school" comparative anatomist. Although he is a jovial fellow who loves to joke, he is deadly serious about his science, and his expression told me that he expected little from what I was going to show him. He told me later that he had been expecting a scrappy little clavicle and a few teeth.

Mischievously enjoying the moment, I reached under the cloth—without lifting it—to pull out the original clavicle that Matthew had found. Peter raised his eyebrows as he handled the small fossil.

"It's fantastic!" he exclaimed.

As I mentioned before, expectations in paleoanthropology run pretty low.

The second fossil I pulled out was the mandible. Peter's face took on an owl-like expression.

"My God," he uttered.

I just smiled as he carefully examined the specimen.

Turning it over in his hand, he said, "The teeth are so small."

I nodded and remained silent. I was eager to hear if his impressions matched with those I had been formulating over the last weeks and months.

"It looks *Homo*-like."

I nodded again, though I added, "Except for the dental proportions. They're primitive."

What I meant was that the teeth had a size pattern different from modern humans. In most people today, the first molar—closest to the front of the mouth—is the largest one. They get smaller as they go farther back in the mouth. The Malapa mandible was the opposite—its back teeth were larger.

"That is australopith-like," Peter agreed.

"There's more," I said. I pulled out a fragment of the humerus, and then the ulna. Peter was dumbstruck as he held first one, then the other of these specimens. To put him out of his misery, I carefully removed the cloth covering the rest of the remains.

Cursing was becoming fairly common in the presence of these fossils in those days.

"Wait until you see the second one," I said, after Peter had recovered. "There's another one?!" He looked at me as if I were mad.

❦

WITH A SMALL CORE team identified, I plotted the way forward. I would need preparators, and that meant money. Malapa was unquestionably a full-time project.

In November, I received a visit from Albert van Jaarsveld, then vice president and managing director of the National Research Foundation of South Africa, the central government funding agency for science. After seeing the skeleton laid out on my desk, he immediately committed emergency funds that would keep the project going for about six months and allow me to hire and begin training my own preparators. His visit was followed by trustees from PAST. They, too, put forward significant emergency funds for the project.

I needed excellent preparators, and I knew I had to build my own team of experts. Celeste Yates, a boisterous South African and a preparator renowned for her patience and skills, was available. I immediately enlisted her to begin working on some of the material.

In those months of late 2008 and early 2009, while I had my whole attention on the fossils from Malapa, the university was merging divisions into a sort of "superinstitute" of paleosciences. In early January a large workshop took place at the university, with guest scientists working to describe the fossil postcranial bones recovered from Sterkfontein over more than 30 years. That work was to culminate in a book-length description of the bones. I thought it was a bad idea, and said so. The idea of producing a monograph seemed so out of date and the science seemed poorly timed. The Little Foot skeleton was obviously important to understanding the Sterkfontein bones, but it was not yet accessible for study. Human evolution is a comparative science, and it was becoming clear that the new fossils from Malapa would be important for understanding Sterkfontein, too. With participants who had little attachment to our university, the workshop seemed like a data-mining exercise with little benefit to South African science. My concerns fell on deaf ears.

So the workshop unfolded without my participation, but I had my hands full with a stream of new discoveries and all the work they required. I took a drive out to Malapa to clear my head. As I stood there above the pit, I put everything else aside. I had enough to do.

# 11

It was mid-January, just after our Christmas break in early 2009, and it was a beautiful summer morning. Back at the lab, the technicians were returning to work, and preparation of the fossils would start up again soon. I had, by then, finished the first high-resolution digital map of the site, and we were ready to begin excavations to recover more material. We needed to start to understand how the blocks containing the skeletons actually went together before the miners had blasted the site.

Soon Peter, Steve, and Darryl would arrive in South Africa to begin work together on the fossils. We needed to compare the Malapa bones systematically with those from other fossil sites, and we booked the fossil vault for several weeks to carry out those comparisons. Together with Job, we would look at the way forward for publication, collaboration with other scientists, and access to the material. I would also look to strengthen these scientists' associations with Wits, building a long-term commitment to support work in South Africa.

As I became increasingly excited about the scientific potential, I returned to the site myself. I stepped down into the pit, going over to the spot where the humerus and scapula had been. Paul Dirks's team of geologists had been out to the site in November 2008, assessing the deposits and removing small samples to attempt to figure out the age of that white line of flowstone—it might be the key to understanding the age of the fossils. I wondered about their results as I looked at the large, empty space where we had removed the big block containing the skeleton. I used my fingers to trace a line above that empty space, which seemed to demarcate some sort of boundary in the rock.

A loose block caught my eye. It was just sitting on the edge of the pit, 20 centimeters or so above where the adult skeleton's arm had been. That rock had somehow gone unnoticed when we collected the big block. I lifted it from the spot where it rested and turned it over in my hands, looking for any fossils. No more than 30 centimeters long, and half again as wide, it probably didn't contain much, I thought.

A small patch of yellow bone caught my attention. I knew its cross section, shaped like a bowling pin. One of the bones prepared last year had been the elbow end of the right humerus of Matthew's child, and I was certain this piece had the same cross section. This broken part would connect to the other, allowing us to refit two parts of the humerus together. Maybe it was all there in the block. That would be a coup.

I took the chunk of breccia back to the lab, but only months later would I find out what secrets that small block actually held.

ᕥ

IN THE HOMININ LAB at Wits, I watched Darryl, Steve, Peter, and Job work on the fossils. They sat with Kris Carlson, whom we had recently added to the team, coming on to play a critical role in the application of technology to the study of the Malapa fossils.

The table was draped in green velvet where the team had arrayed the Malapa skeletons alongside dozens of casts of fossils from other sites across Africa. Two weeks of work together had brought us all toward one key question: What were they?

"So, is everyone leaning toward this being *Homo*?" I asked. Everyone paused their work and looked at me.

"Tobias seemed to think so," Darryl said. "And if he's convinced, that would go a long way toward convincing others."

Phillip Tobias had dropped in to the lab a few days earlier. Showing emotion as he handled the fossils, he noted how small the teeth and mandible seemed to be in comparison to *Australopithecus*. He declared it "*Homo habilis*–like." He would know, we all thought, because he had, after all, been one of the authors of the original description of *habilis* with Louis Leakey and John Napier back in 1964. His was not an opinion to be taken lightly.

We had easily eliminated the fossils' being *robustus*. That species was easily recognized from its teeth—the very large molars; the tiny incisors and canines; the premolar teeth that, in humans, are small, two-cusped affairs but are nearly the size of molars in *robustus*. There would be no mistaking the teeth in front of us: They did not come from a robust australopith.

The question really came down to this: Were these remains better placed in the genus *Homo* or in the genus *Australopithecus*?

It was a timeless question. Tobias had asked it with Louis Leakey in 1964 when they defined *Homo habilis*. For many months after the *habilis* fossils were discovered, Phillip had resisted calling them *Homo,* noting their similarities with the South African *Australopithecus africanus*. Phillip faced the question again in 1976, when Alun Hughes and his workers uncovered a skull at Sterkfontein known as Stw 53. This skull shared several features with the *habilis* skulls from East Africa, and came from some of the latest Sterkfontein deposits, which contained rudimentary stone tools like those from Olduvai Gorge, but scientists have argued over the skull ever since. *Homo* or *Australopithecus*? Richard Leakey had faced the question with his discovery of the KNM-ER 1470 skull in 1972, the skull that he saw as a complete skull of *Homo habilis* but that a later scientist would put into a species of its own, *Homo rudolfensis*. Don Johanson faced the question in 1974 with his teeth from Hadar, in which he saw similarities with *Homo,* and the Lucy skeleton: In the end he placed both together into *Australopithecus*. Meave Leakey, too, had faced the question in 1999 with a fossil skull from the Lomekwi site, west of Lake Turkana. That skull had similarities to some *Homo* specimens, especially the 1470 skull—yet it was different, sharing more features with primitive species like *afarensis*. Her team placed the enigmatic skull into a genus all its own, *Kenyanthropus platyops*.

Now, it was our turn to face this question. The answer would not come easy. We first had to compare the new Malapa fossils with the fossils that had been unearthed at Sterkfontein over the years. Since the early days of Robert Broom's discoveries at the site, Sterkfontein had become a key problem for understanding human evolution. Paleoanthropologists recognized nearly all the Sterkfontein fossils as representing just one species, *Australopithecus africanus.*

But the Sterkfontein fossils represented a lot of diversity. If you went to excavate a cemetery full of the bones of modern humans, you would almost never find such large differences among individuals as we could see among the Sterkfontein fossils. They must have accumulated at this site for many thousands of years, probably from many populations. Maybe there was even more than one species there—certainly others had suggested as such—but the jury was still out.

Looking at our Malapa jaw, we could not easily lump it with any of the others. But it was hard to be sure.

We had *Homo* fossils in the vault to compare it with. Tobias had called the Stw 53 skull *Homo habilis,* although other scientists disagreed. As Tobias saw it, its brain was a bit bigger than that of the australopiths, and its face a bit shorter, squared off a bit at the front just below its nose. But we hadn't found those parts of the Malapa skeletons yet.

We were looking at a treasure trove of new fossils—two partial skeletons. But they were nearly all postcranial bones. For the entire history of paleoanthropology in Africa, scientists had focused their attention primarily on the skulls and teeth. Mostly, that was what they had found. So far our skeletons were missing these parts, except for the two isolated teeth and the mandible. Those pieces were *Homo*-like, as Tobias had confirmed. But how could we test that hypothesis with the rest of the skeletons when there were hardly any other fossils of early *Homo* to compare them against?

"We need a skull," Darryl lamented.

I nodded. A skull would help.

"And we need to go look at all of the *Homo* material in East Africa," Job added.

# 12

The air scribes with their tiny jackhammer tips were silent one morning in late April 2009 as I worked my way from prep station to prep station, looking at the previous evening's results. I was particularly eager to see what Pepson Makanela, one of our top preparators, had done. He had been working on the new block I recovered from the site in January.

The small cross section of bone I had spotted was near the end of a humerus, and it did mirror the break in the part of the child's arm we already had. Pepson had been carefully working on this arm bone, exposing more and more of the shaft. If it was complete, it would give us a direct comparison of the juvenile's arm with the adult's, telling us a lot about how the two skeletons might differ, and maybe even about the growth and development of these hominins.

Sitting down in the empty chair at Pepson's station to get a closer look at how his work had progressed, I saw something that I didn't expect. There, just off to the side of the humerus shaft, about three-quarters of the way up the arm, a new patch of fossil bone shone light against the darker rock that surrounded it. I recognized it immediately—it was a tiny window onto a fossil maxilla—the part of the face just above the canine tooth.

A face would be a tremendously important find for us. It might be just what we needed to give us a broader comparison with skulls of *Homo*. As it lay there in the rock, I was fairly certain it would only be a fragment, though. The block was so small. Still, a fragment was better than nothing at all.

When Pepson arrived for work, I asked him to concentrate on this small area, to expose a bit more, and to be particularly careful about the delicate areas of the face that he was approaching. I showed him a cast of the Taung Child's face so he would know what he might expect. I checked back on his progress throughout the day. As the careful preparation progressed, it became clear that quite a lot of the face was there. The excitement grew in the prep lab. A stream of scientists and students stopped by, watching as first the base of the eye socket was revealed and then, by the end of the day, a tooth row began to emerge. Gleaming white teeth in exceptional condition—I was thrilled!

I brought Jackie and the kids to the lab on Saturday to show them our newest discovery. I took a few family photos of the three of them posing with the newest addition to our family, and then I showed them what I thought was preserved in the block. I was pretty confident it would be half of a face, and I used the cast of the Taung Child's skull to demonstrate how the Malapa child's face must be sitting within the rock.

"I can tell you how much is in there," Jackie said confidently.

I turned to her with curiosity. My wife, Jackie, is a radiologist with access to a CT scanner, which uses x-rays to look inside things, taking snapshots from many angles that are then reconstructed by the computer into either black and gray slices of sections through a body or, with the right software, a ghostly three-dimensional image. But medical CT scanners use relatively weak beams, protecting human patients from possible harm. Sticking rocks into these scanners had never been very effective because they were so much denser than living bone, with a bit of metal content, leaving a useless image with no real detail. I had tried it numerous times over the years and always failed. For that reason, I had never even considered trying CT on the dense Malapa material.

"We have a new scanner that I think can penetrate that rock and give good results," she continued.

"Can we try Monday?" I asked, eagerly. If we could see into the rock, it would certainly help with decisions about how to prepare the precious fossil.

Monday morning, Jackie and I sat in a darkened room before a computer screen. Calling up the black-and-white image of the block, she picked a random slice somewhere near the center and adjusted the contrast for the best focus. As the image began to resolve itself at her skilled hands, my mouth literally dropped open. Jackie had picked a slice that directly passed through a point almost where the midline of the face would be.

There, as clear as a photograph, was the cross section of a complete skull!

My mind raced through the fossil record, thinking about the hominin fossil skulls I knew, most reconstructed from hundreds of tiny fragments. Such fossils were often highly distorted, buried under tons of rock, often crushed or trampled even before the sediment had enclosed them. As Jackie and I scrolled through the remarkably clear images, we realized that we were not looking at a fragmented or distorted skull. The image before us appeared to be an almost perfectly complete, undistorted juvenile skull with all its teeth intact. It seemed almost miraculous that something like this could have been preserved. Here we had a skull together with much of its skeleton, and the skeleton of a second individual besides.

❧

THIS SKULL WOULD PROVE to be the key to understanding what the Malapa hominins were and what they were not. Using the new CT images as a guide, the preparators slowly revealed the face. Fossil after fossil followed as we worked our way through the Malapa material. First, another mandible, which must belong to the adult skeleton. Then more vertebrae and pelvic bones from both individuals. As we added one piece after another to their anatomies, the portraits were becoming clearer.

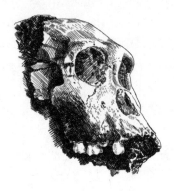

*The Malapa skull only partially prepared*
*from the surrounding matrix*

By midyear, we knew that the child was probably a male. His still growing body was almost the size of the adult skeleton, which, by the same logic, was probably a female. The small canine tooth of the adult suggested a female, too. If this child had been a human, the development of bones and teeth would make us think he was between around 9 and 13 years old when he died. We could not, at this stage, know exactly how fast these early hominin individuals would have grown up, but comparisons from other immature fossil specimens gave some reason to think that they grew up faster than children today. As we built the two skeletons, piece by piece, we decided to give them each a unique designation, to assist us in talking about them. We called the male child "MH1," short for "Malapa Hominid 1." The second skeleton naturally became "MH2."

The complete skull was what we had wanted to help figure out what these skeletons were. But even with all that new information, we still weren't sure whether this child was *Homo, Australopithecus,* or something else. The skull was small. With a brain around 420 cubic centimeters in size, it was similar to skulls of australopith species, including *Australopithecus africanus.* It was smaller than any specimen of *Homo* except for that of the Flores skeleton, and controversial as that was, it couldn't help much with our decision. Brain size had always been seen as a key distinguishing feature of our genus, but even after decades of searching across the whole of Africa, few of the earliest representatives of *Homo* had any evidence of brain size at all. *Homo habilis* and *Homo rudolfensis* merited their place with brains between around 600 and 800 cubic centimeters in size, but no fossil from earlier than around two million years ago preserved such evidence. Some earlier finds had been named *Homo* over the years, but always on the basis of teeth and jaws. And the teeth and jaws of this little skull were indeed the most *Homo*-like of its features. As the skull emerged from the rock, its face showed us something different from *africanus* faces, something a bit more human. Our basic problem was that the fossil record of early *Homo* was much less complete than the Malapa skeletons.

I arranged a trip for the entire team to travel up to East Africa in September, thinking that the direct comparison with the East African fossils assigned to both genera would help us identify the Malapa species once and for all. Meanwhile, the geologists and geochronologists had been busy. They had thrown every possible method at the problem of getting a date for the fossils. There were, by that time, two geological teams working in parallel. One team was using geophysical methods to date the sediments and flowstones that surrounded the bones. The other team was examining the fossil fauna, to try to identify extinct species found nearby that might help estimate the age of the deposits. These two independent streams of research would eventually join to create what we hoped would be an accurate age estimate for the Malapa fossils.

Paul Dirks, Jan Kramers, and Robyn Pickering focused their energies on trying to date the white flowstones, using a method that Jan and Robyn had worked on for years—uranium-lead dating. The uranium-lead dating technique assesses two separate radioactive decay chains: uranium-238 decaying to lead-206, termed the "uranium series," and uranium-235 decaying to lead-207, the "actinium series." Minute quantities of the two types of uranium became part of the calcite crystals within flowstones when they were originally laid down. The chain of decay of these uranium isotopes into the different isotopes of lead provides a way to estimate the age of the flowstone formation. We were in luck at Malapa—the geological team found that there was a flowstone that could be studied with this technique near the fossil hominins. Combining these findings with studies of the fauna found near the hominin skeletons, we could estimate the age of the skeletons: two million years old.

So now we had an approximate age for the fossil skeletons, but we still needed to decide what they were.

# 13

We could feel the depth of the history in the fossil vault of Kenya's Nairobi National Museums. A high-domed ceiling keeps the interior cool, and the cabinets around the walls are filled with treasures from decades of hunting for fossil hominins. Louis and Mary Leakey used the museum, then known as the Coryndon, as a base of operations for nearly two decades before striking fossil gold at Olduvai Gorge, Tanzania, in the late 1950s. Their fossil finds were still housed here. Their son Richard followed in their footsteps, claiming his place in the pantheon of great fossil finders by leading his famed "hominid gang" on expeditions largely around Lake Turkana, in northern Kenya. On both the east and west sides of this tremendous, jade-colored lake, Richard, later joined by his wife, Meave, and their colleagues, had picked up and excavated hundreds of remains of hominins.

Some of those fossils represented very early branches of the genus *Homo,* and that was why we had come. Emma Mbua, curator of the collections, had kindly arranged for our team to view these wonderful collections on relatively short notice. We found ourselves seated around the large table in a laboratory adjacent to the vault—boxes of fossils set out in an orderly manner around the table, casts of the Malapa fossils distributed in a less orderly fashion. The work progressed well for almost a week, as we worked through the greater part of the East African fossil hominin record, carefully comparing every specimen with the relevant counterpart from Malapa.

Actually handling the original fossils attributed to early *Homo* held by the Kenya National Museums had me beginning to doubt my convictions. I had fairly convinced myself back in South Africa that the Malapa hominins belonged in our genus, *Homo*. Those first looks at the short *Homo*-like face of the Malapa fossil skull—so different from the long snouts of the South African australopiths—had put me in that frame of mind. The molar and premolar teeth of these fossils were mostly small, too—and didn't those small teeth suggest an improved, more humanlike diet? We had worked with the casts of many of these fossils, but casts are often based on scientists' reconstructions, and they can therefore be misleading. As I handled these original fossils, I was seeing more and more differences between the Malapa material and the fossils currently understood to belong in the genus *Homo*. Everyone else on the team was coming to the same conclusions.

There was that small brain—that certainly didn't seem very *Homo*-like. Phillip Tobias had helped Louis Leakey define *Homo habilis*, focusing on the larger brains of the Olduvai Gorge skulls compared with those of the australopiths. Now, examining those very fossils, we could see that the cranial pieces of some of those *habilis* fossils curved gently, suggesting a brain size more like a grapefruit. Our Malapa skull was no bigger than an orange.

Still, here was a fossil skull of *habilis* found much later, at Koobi Fora, one of Richard Leakey's trove of fossils collected in the 1970s. KNM-ER 1813 was the smallest *habilis* skull on record, with a brain size just over 500 cubic centimeters. That was still larger than our Malapa skull, but that face—with its short vertical profile—was not so different. Besides, because people had begun to accept the Flores skeleton as *Homo floresiensis*, brain size didn't seem quite so important in defining *Homo* anymore. Maybe the Malapa skull wasn't too small for *Homo* after all.

One thing was clear to all of us: Not one of the skulls, jaws, or teeth we were seeing in Kenya was a match for the features of those from Malapa. There were some strange ones there in the Nairobi museum vault: a skull with a small crest on its top for its big jaw muscles, but smaller teeth than any robust skull should have; a short, square *Homo*-like jaw with tremendous teeth; a classic *habilis* mandible with long, long wisdom teeth. We looked closely at every one of them, and each time we found that they just didn't seem to fit what we had in the Malapa fossils. Our fossils were not what had been called *Homo habilis,* nor *rudolfensis,* nor did they really look like any of the pieces here that might belong to some form of *Australopithecus.* They were something new.

We carried out the work for days, debating back and forth among ourselves. Each day, our discussion would carry over into the evening, when we adjourned from the museum to a local bar, hashing out the day's work over cold Tusker beers.

"Tomorrow, I want to perform an experiment," I said one evening. "Let's pull all of the characteristics out of our studies and list them as australopith-like or *Homo*-like, and go through each one by one. Also, let's settle on what our definition of a genus actually is."

This was easier said than done. Species were, in a way, pretty clear. In living animals, biologists look at species in terms of interbreeding: If populations can interbreed with each other in their natural habitat, they belong to the same species. Of course, with fossil animals, that's not possible—if we wait for two fossils to interbreed, we'll be waiting a very long time. So, paleontologists look at whether a fossil has unique features not seen in other fossils, and compare combinations of features with the skeletons of living populations of animals. These comparisons are not always simple, though, and they are made even harder with a fossil sample like those from Sterkfontein. With so many fragments that might cover thousands of years of time, one could imagine those remains representing a single evolving species.

But we were finding the Malapa case to be easier. There just weren't any other fossils, neither from South Africa nor from East Africa, showing the same pattern of features we saw in these two skeletons. The fact that they were skeletons, not fragmentary jaws or a single skull, gave us confidence.

The arms of these fossils were very long, and we had leg bones to show their relative sizes. We had, by now, a heel bone, and although the ankle and femur both clearly showed that the Malapa individuals were upright walking creatures, that heel had a very strange, twisted look, almost like that of a chimpanzee. The pelvis parts were not broad and flared like Lucy's, but a bit more compact, like a human's. It wasn't just that we couldn't match all the features of the skull, jaws, and teeth of Malapa to any other skull we had seen. If we had hypothesized that any of those other fossils, however fragmentary, represented the same strange mix of features found in the Malapa skeletons, people would have thought we were dreaming. No, clearly they came from a species new to science.

Deciding on a genus posed a harder problem, because different biologists give different meanings to the term. Linnaeus invented the system that biologists still use to classify species, and he used the idea of a genus to mark species that look like each other and have similar habits of life—biologists today call this idea "adaptive grade." A hundred years later, Darwin showed that species have common origins. To biologists, this means that the members of a genus should be related to each other—that they share an ancestor. On a tree of relationships, they belong to a single branch, what biologists call a "clade." But some branches of the tree of life include species that adapt to their environments in different ways, and it's not always easy to tell whether species that look similar are really closely related to each other. A species can evolve rapidly, gaining a new set of adaptations that relate to its environment in a new way, making it look different from its relatives. Grade and clade may not match.

In 1960, Louis and Mary Leakey had found the first specimens of *Homo habilis* at Olduvai Gorge. For more than 40 years since, it had stood as the earliest known member of the genus *Homo,* a species that set a new evolutionary course that led to *Homo sapiens,* people living today. When he enlisted Phillip Tobias and John Napier to define the new species, Louis Leakey had to decide on a boundary line separating our genus from its ancestors. They based the idea of *Homo* upon a common set of adaptations.

Tool use, more humanlike hands, a larger brain, smaller teeth—all these things together indicated a new pattern of life, one that set our ancestors on a human path. If these scientists were right, these features that define the *Homo* pattern of adaptation should also define one branch. Grade and clade should be one and the same.

But in more recent years, some scientists have challenged this idea. What we knew about the body of *habilis,* with its small size, suggested that maybe this creature did not use the environment in the same way later kinds of *Homo* did. It could not have been routinely walking long distances and using large areas of the landscape in the way that the larger *Homo erectus* and later humans had done. The smaller brain of *habilis* pointed in the same direction. The way *habilis* interacted with its environment might have been a lot more like *Australopithecus.* And if *habilis* got reassigned out of the genus *Homo,* a lot of the more fragmentary fossils proposed as candidates for the earliest known members of the genus would have to go, too. Whatever their places on the family tree— which no one really could say for sure—the adaptive grade of these fossils was not the same.

So, understanding the origin of our genus was a big question in the study of human evolution, and we were caught in the middle of it. These Malapa fossils were what they were—whatever we called them wouldn't change that—and whether they were placed in *Homo* or not, they would provide new evidence of what the ancestors of *Homo* had been like. But the name might shape the way other scientists test hypotheses about *Homo* and its origin—and the way they might respond when we revealed these new fossils from Malapa. The same features that argued for understanding the Malapa fossils as a new species actually created a big problem for us as we tried to assign them to a genus. The mixture of traits included many that had been found in *Australopithecus* fossils and many others that had been found in *Homo* fossils. How could we decide between the two?

The next day found me in front of a flip board, pen in hand, before the whole team. I created two columns: "Primitive" and "Derived."

Primitive features were those shared with the distant relatives and ancestors of *Homo,* whereas derived features were those shared with humans or closer human relatives, such as *Homo erectus.* "OK," I said. "Let's start at the head."

One by one we went through the features. The tiny brain of the Malapa hominins, at 420 cubic centimeters, went under "Primitive." The size of the teeth, "Derived." And on and on. Down the body, to the foot, we explored and debated each bit of morphology before placing it in a column. We then repeated the exercise, but with two different headings: "*Australopithecus*" and "Early *Homo.*" During the course of making this list, we batted back and forth ideas about how to define a genus, and we finally decided that we would focus on the adaptive grade idea: physical characteristics and abilities, not common ancestors. It was, in a way, an inevitable choice. We had some of the best evidence across the entire skeleton for how these animals interacted with their environment. But despite their many similarities with some other species of *Homo,* we could not say for sure that they were close relatives on the family tree. That would take more evidence from other fossil species, evidence we didn't have.

At the end of several hours, I stepped back, scanning the two long lists. I nodded to myself before looking to the group. "OK, I'm convinced," I said. "It shares a lot of features with early *Homo,* but it's not that. It's *Australopithecus.*"

There was a sigh of relief. I think several members of the team thought I was going to push for these hominins being early *Homo,* just because it seems sexier than *Australopithecus.* The lists were nearly equal in length, but we could all see that this hominin was not a long-distance walker, and its long arms appeared to be adapted to climbing. With its small brain, I just couldn't see placing it in the genus *Homo.* The evidence was what it was.

That evening, sitting at a restaurant, Steve Churchill asked me the question that I think was on the minds of several members of the Malapa team: "What would it take for you to put a hominin like this one into *Homo?*"

I thought for a moment of the long debates and discussions held over the last many months. "If it had long legs and humanlike feet, I could disregard the brain size."

Little did I know that in just a few years, I would face exactly this question, but with an entirely new set of bones.

# 14

Because we had found a new species, we needed to give it a name. Taking a break from looking at the fossils, I played around with the Sesotho dictionary on my laptop, trying out words that might have meaning for either the fossils or the site. Occasionally I would speak one out loud for the group who were there, silently working on the fossils. They developed a ritual—thumbs down, not even looking up as they expressed dissatisfaction with one name after another.

Finally, I looked for the Sesotho word for "spring," as in a source of water. We suspected that the Malapa site might have been a water source that had attracted these hominins and other animals, causing them to fall to their deaths. In Sesotho, the word for "spring" also means "wellspring," "fountain," or "source": *sediba*.

I said the word out loud and everyone stopped and looked at me. "I like it. What does it mean?" asked Darryl.

I explained the meaning. First Job then each of the others nodded in agreement.

"At least a BBC presenter won't mispronounce it!" I said, only half-joking. We had our name: *Australopithecus sediba*.

We made the first public announcement of the new species in April 2010, in the august journal *Science*. Our announcement describing the fossils noted them as representing a new *Homo*-like species of *Australopithecus*. The scientific work showed in detail the mosaic nature of *sediba*'s anatomy—features

seen in several other known hominin species yet never in this combination—
and how it appeared to represent a transition between more primitive australopiths and the earliest members of the genus *Homo*. It was a time of
celebration for everyone involved in the discovery, as the work received
headlines around the world. Twenty months after Matthew had shouted,
"Dad, I found a fossil!" we had now published the first scientific description
of two partial skeletons of a new hominin species.

We could not be sure exactly how *sediba* was related to humans on our
family tree. Our study of the features of the skull, jaws, and teeth made it
clear that *sediba* was very close to the branch that led to *Homo*. That branch
included not only extinct species like *habilis* and *erectus*, but modern humans
too. Its similarities to these species made it possible that something like *sediba*
might have actually given rise to our genus. Certainly we could not rule it
out. Neither could we rule out that *sediba* had evolved for a long time in
parallel with *Homo*. The common ancestor of the two forms might be very
different from either.

Science journalists sometimes treat human evolution like a horse race,
describing how different fossil discoveries are jockeying for a position as
the true ancestor of humanity. It is a tendency that goes back to the Taung
Child discovery and even earlier, a mistake sometimes made by scientists
as well as journalists. We could not dismiss the possibility that *sediba* might
be an ancestor of *Homo*, and this proved controversial. Other scientists had
claimed much earlier evidence of *Homo*, or *Homo*-like relatives, dating back
to 2.5 million years ago or even more. This was earlier than the geological
age of the Malapa skeletons, which were only around two million years old.
To some scientists, the age of the skeletons was enough to answer the question by itself. *Sediba* might look like a human ancestor in some ways, but
it was just too recent. This was a simple argument, the idea that ancestors
must be older than their descendants. But in fact, we didn't know how old
*sediba* might be; we only knew how old the Malapa skeletons were. The
species existed for some time, and the evidence didn't say when that time
started or ended.

What we could say was that *sediba*'s anatomy was an unexpected mosaic, and that had big consequences for the way we understood the origin of *Homo*. Even the most exceptional skulls of *habilis* and *rudolfensis* fossils had no arms or legs accompanying them. What little anyone thought they knew about the rest of the *habilis* skeleton, it looked like an australopith, and no one had ever found a *rudolfensis* skeleton. Most scientists called these skulls *Homo* because they had a slightly bigger brain than most australopiths, with a less massive jawbone and jaw muscles. But most fossils of early *Homo* didn't even preserve that much evidence: We might have a single piece of a jaw, a part of a skull, or a handful of teeth. Looking at such a fragment, it is natural to assume it belongs to a human or australopith skeleton as we know them. A fragment of *Homo*-like jawbone would have belonged to a *Homo*-like body, with a *Homo*-like brain size. For some scientists, a jaw that looked like *Homo* should be evidence that the ancient individual belonged to *Homo*, whatever the rest of the body might say.

With the Malapa skeletons we had vastly more evidence from across much of the body, and yet we found that different pieces of evidence conflicted with the idea that any one part could predict *sediba*'s relationships. What if we had only found a part of the jawbone? What if we had found only part of the pelvis? Both these parts were more like *Homo* than other parts of the skeleton, like the legs, feet, or shoulders. If we had only a fragment, our conclusion could hardly help but be different from what the whole skeletons told us.

Because we weren't sure, we felt it was important to be cautious claiming anything about *sediba*'s place in our evolution. We would need a lot more fossil evidence to test such ideas. Our team launched into the work of understanding how the different parts of *sediba* worked, and how they might fit together into a story about how this species had evolved.

This first description of the new species, which made the cover of *Science* magazine, was just the beginning of our work. Over the next several years, two special editions of *Science* magazine dedicated to *sediba*, each with a cover image of Malapa fossils, would appear. In 2011, our team published papers describing in detail the form of the brain, hand, foot, and pelvis.

We also were able to refine the date of the fossils, placing them at a very precise 1.977 million years ago. The two skeletons had been sandwiched between two layers of white flowstone, and we discovered that these, in fact, represented the same short span of time that groundwater was depositing the calcite in the cave. By coincidence, a reversal of Earth's magnetic poles had occurred during the thousand years or so that these flowstones had been forming. This magnetic event allowed our geochronologists to narrow the time between those flowstones to a very small window. Our next series of scientific papers, published in 2013, described more of the upper limb, spine, and mandible, and something about how *sediba* must have walked with its humanlike pelvis and strange heel.

Luckily, we were able to satisfy the extraordinary amount of interest in and coverage of our science thanks to the fast pace of new research on the Malapa discovery. By this time, almost a hundred scientists were engaged in different aspects of the work on *sediba*. The team had grown rapidly because the fossils raised so many new questions that required different kinds of expertise to answer. It also grew rapidly because, even before the public announcement of the discovery, I had set the stage for open access to the fossil material. With a significant find of my own, I could create a program of research in any way my colleagues and I saw fit. My instinct was to open the fossils for any scientist to study, and soon dozens had begun to engage in the science, working with our team.

After the *sediba* publications, other paleoanthropologists sometimes criticized our team for publishing research too quickly. Such criticism may seem hard to take seriously, because we published our first description of the fossils almost two years after Matthew's first discovery, hardly a sprint. Our team's open process led to a much wider array of research than a few colleagues and I would have managed by ourselves, and over the next eight years the research led to dozens of publications by our team and other independent scientists. By taking this approach, we have been able to put our conclusions repeatedly to the highest test: open inspection by the field at large. Publishing scientific work is the way that scientists communicate about data. It is the normal way that science advances. That scientific philosophy does differ starkly from a small fraction of paleoanthropologists who work in comparative secrecy for many years on new discoveries, sometimes laboring alone or in small close-knit groups. But in science, we do not accept conclusions because they are faster or slower, whether they take months or decades. We accept conclusions that are supported by data, data that other scientists can see and replicate.

Making the fossils more open to study meant making copies of the fossils available. As early as 2009, I set up a casting program to create replicas of the Malapa remains with just this in mind. We distributed these first casts to colleagues involved in the descriptions, but then to major museums around the world that housed other hominin fossils. The goal was simple: Put a set of casts of *sediba* in every major museum in the world that had an interest in studying hominin evolution. With the assistance of the South African government, we pretty much accomplished this by 2013.

THE 2011 ANNUAL MEETING of the American Association of Physical Anthropologists (AAPA) took place in Minneapolis. I carried two large, black gun cases to the meeting, packed with casts of every fossil of the two *sediba* skeletons. I let as many people see the casts as possible, so they could review the scientific findings by looking at replicas of the real fossils instead of simply trusting what we had written. As our scientific colleagues crowded around the open cases, they had to react to what their eyes told them instead of relying upon what they assumed they already knew. It sounds incredible now, more than five years later, to think that this strategy was practically unheard of at the time. I had brought new fossils from Malapa that our team had not yet published, material that only insiders at other fossil sites might ever have the chance to see. It was so unusual, science reporters at the meetings picked up on the story, and wrote not just about the fossil casts and their implications but also about the openness with which I was sharing my finds.

I donated a full set of the Malapa casts to the association, on the condition that it make them available every year. At the 2012 AAPA meeting, we organized a session in which other museums and institutions also provided casts of their fossil hominins. In this case, we included nothing that had not already been published from other fossil sites, but this still included many copies of fossils that were nowhere available for purchase and were not in teaching collections.

The session was a huge success. Scientists and students packed the room, crowding around tables with copies of fossils they had never seen in person. The *sediba* fossils, along with fossils from other sites around the world, gave rise to intense discussions among specialists who had never been involved in paleoanthropology before. Many of these experts in human biology or anthropology had avoided the study of human evolution because they would not be allowed to see fossil material. One surprise was how popular the table holding the casts of the little Lucy skeleton turned out to be. Even though it had been found nearly 40 years before, many of the anthropologists had only seen it in photos or in museums, and had never been able to examine a copy firsthand. Something in our discipline was shifting, and it seemed as if *sediba* was the start of it.

# PART III

# Finding *naledi*

❦

# 15

In August 2013, I leaned back in my office chair, staring at the dots scattered across the Google Earth map. It had been five years since the Malapa discovery—one among many of those dots representing the entrances to caves or former caves that had lost their roofs and now left breccia exposed on the landscape.

Work at Malapa had stopped for the moment while a large protective structure was being assembled at the site. Ultimately called the Beetle, this structure would perch over the little site like a giant insect, offering a platform for the excavators and protecting the site from the elements. Until it was finished, our team would not be able to work on-site. Much of the team was occupied completing the final research papers on the *sediba* material anyway. Things were coming to a natural pause—and I was itching to go exploring again.

I had surveyed the sites shown by all of those dots on the map back in 2008, but I wanted a second look. There were new caves there. I had done an underground search with some of my caving buddies in the 1990s as part of the Atlas Project, but we hadn't come up with much. Now I suspected there were hundreds of underground systems we hadn't seen. These dots were doorways to an underworld, with potential new discoveries.

Just then, someone knocked on my office door. It was Pedro Boshoff, wearing a red knit cap with a bobble on top and clutching his hands in front of himself. He was also barefoot. For the many years I had known him, Pedro had always hated shoes.

Pedro was a former student of mine who had planned to write his master's thesis on how hyenas use caves but who had vanished years before without finishing the degree. I knew he had gone off diamond mining in central and West Africa, because he had dropped in once a few years back and told me about the slim fruits of that labor. He had also been one of my caving buddies back in the 1990s.

"What can I do for you?" I asked.

Pedro looked like he was about to cry. "May I speak with you for a minute?"

That conversation stretched to over an hour. Diamond prospecting had failed him. He lamented leaving paleoanthropology years before—it was a mistake, and could I possibly do anything for him?

I watched Pedro carefully as he spoke. I knew he had the skills for underground work. Besides being ex-military, he was a longtime member of the local caving society. He had been lucky in finding fossils before and had actually discovered the first hominin teeth at the new site of Drimolen back in 1994, although circumstances had kept him from being recognized for that discovery.

His appearance at just that moment seemed serendipitous. I wasn't entirely confident that Pedro might not up and disappear again, and I didn't have any funds for exploration at the moment, but here was someone who could find fossils, and I thought he deserved a chance. I had enough reserves in my budget, and so I offered him an exploration job. After he had left, I called my laboratory manager, Bonita de Klerk, into the office. "I want you to contact procurement and see how I might go about buying a motorcycle through the university," I told her. Bonita had become tolerant of my odd requests over the years, but this one left her shaking her head.

Two weeks later, Pedro was back in my office to report on his first efforts, motorcycle helmet in hand. I had asked him to start first in the Sterkfontein Valley. My experience discovering Malapa, such a short distance away from where I had spent 17 years digging at Gladysvale, had taught me a lesson. The places you think you know best might surprise you.

But Pedro had found that the caves in the area were full of narrow, tight passages, and the years had added some kilos to his frame. It was also too dangerous to work alone. "I want to bring on some amateurs," he said. "I've met these two youngsters, Rick Hunter and Steven Tucker. They are good guys, pretty new to caving, but I can trust them."

I nodded as I listened. I had not enlisted amateur assistance in exploration before, and I was asking Pedro to do work that was a specialized skill. But if we were going into unexplored areas of caves, we needed people with the right physical build to get into the deeper systems. Pedro was also right that caving alone was dangerous and downright stupid. I made a snap decision. "OK, show them what we're after and send them out."

Weeks went by, August into September. Pedro would call me with updates, or drop by my office with reports of their frequent caving trips. He was dividing the search between sites to the west, in the vicinity of Sterkfontein, and locations farther east, where he had a hunch there were new things to find. Steven and Rick seemed to be working out great. They were evidently keen on joining the project and ready to go out any night they could after work.

On September 14, my cell phone rang. It was Pedro. "Rick and Steven think they found something good!"

People have approached me many times over the years with reports of finding some great thing, and it usually turns out to be less than advertised. But you never know for sure, so I always take the time to at least look at photos. "Bring me pictures," I said, hanging up and promptly forgetting about the conversation as I moved on to editing a *sediba* manuscript.

Two more weeks passed, with occasional updates from Pedro, and I heard nothing more about Steven and Rick's purported discovery until the last day of September. Pedro again called me. Rick and Steven have pictures, he said, and he was going to meet up with them to take a look. I gave him appropriate words of encouragement and hung up, not giving the call another thought.

❧

I T WAS NINE O'CLOCK at night on October 1, and I sat at home at my kitchen counter, finishing off the day's emails. It had been a long day for me at Malapa, visiting the construction of the Beetle, and when I got home I turned off my cell phone. The buzz of the front gate intercom surprised me. We almost never had visitors that late at night. I could see the headlights of a car shining through the gate as I curiously picked up the receiver.

"You're going to want to let us in!"

It was Pedro. I will admit now that the strange tone in his voice gave me a few seconds of hesitation about letting "us" in, whoever that was, but a few minutes later Pedro was standing in my dining room with a tall, skinny man with brown, unkempt hair.

So this was Steven. Pedro introduced us hastily, his body language telegraphing his excitement.

"So what do you have?" I asked.

Steven quickly flipped open his laptop and brought a picture up on the screen. There, upon a piece of dirty map paper, was a hominin mandible. A cloth measuring tape next to it gave scale. It wasn't human; that much was clear. The teeth were in the wrong proportions to be from any recent population. A second image showed more bones, all seemingly hominin. A third showed a rounded, broken white outline in the dirt floor of the cave. It was the right shape to be the cross section of a skull—a tiny skull.

Steven swears I cursed. Might be. By this point in my life, though, I thought I knew better than that.

The pictures, Steven explained, were from a well-explored and well-mapped series of connected cave systems called Empire cave and Rising Star cave. On September 13, Steven and Rick had climbed a large underground rockfall called the Dragon's Back. When they reached the top, they found a jagged slot that narrowed to a pinch point 18 centimeters wide. I've learned that cavers like Steven and Rick look at such narrow openings as opportunities. Steven went in first, and then Rick followed. The squeeze was tight, vertical, and almost 12 meters to the bottom. Luckily for them, it didn't open up to leave them dangling from the ceiling of a large cavern. A small drop of a couple meters to the bottom, and they found themselves in a chamber. On the floor they found bones, many bones, lying loose there on the floor. Some looked to them like the sort of bones we were after.

But their camera didn't work.

It had taken them hours of exploration to find this spot, but out they had climbed, up the narrow slot and down the Dragon's Back, retracing their tortuous path in. This was the discovery they had told Pedro about two weeks earlier. Now they had managed to get back in, and they had made sure the camera worked this time.

I was completely speechless for a moment, flipping back and forth through the pictures. Finally I began to ask questions. I quizzed Steven deeply about the situation of this find. I noticed white areas on the fossils, suggesting some recent damage to them. Steven swore that he and Rick had not done this and had been very careful. He also mentioned that there was a small survey marker on the back wall of the chamber, left by a caver sometime before, who knows when. Whoever it was had not noted the chamber on any map of the cave.

I truly couldn't believe what I was seeing. Fossil hominin remains just lying on the floor of a cave? It seemed impossible. I got up to get us some beers. Jackie, Megan, and Matthew wandered downstairs to see what the commotion was about. They couldn't believe those images either. It was nothing short of incredible.

# 16

I slid first one booted foot, then the next into the legs of the one-piece overalls. There was just enough room to get my shoes through each leg without making a complete fool of myself by falling over in an unbalanced heap. Pulling the jumpsuit up proved less difficult as I slipped my arms through the sleeves, all under the critical eye of John Dickie, an officer of the caving club. Pedro, Steven, Rick, and a few other members of the club looked on, having already kitted themselves up at what seemed like lightning speed.

It was late at night, four days after Rick, Steven, and Pedro had shown me the photos of the cave. This was the first time both Rick and Steven could be available for a return trip to the site, both having day jobs. Steven was an accountant by day, studying for his professional exams. Rick was a card-carrying member of Mensa who had almost been kicked out of high school due to an incident involving an explosion and a chemistry lab—you cannot make this stuff up—and now moved from one construction job to another. Both Steven and Rick had the sinewy frames that often characterize really great cavers: They were what I often refer to as being "physiologically appropriate" for such work.

Dave Ingold, a wiry septuagenarian and longtime caver, looked me over with a critical eye. I felt like I was being judged in a way I hadn't experienced since my childhood days competing in livestock shows back in Sylvania, Georgia. "He'll fit," Dave said with a grin and then a chuckle.

I raised my eyebrows. I didn't intend to try the 18-centimeter slot; my head alone was probably too big to fit. But could the route through the cave up to that point be so narrow that they were worried about me fitting? I glanced over at my son, Matthew, who had kitted up as fast as the others. Now 14, he was more than six feet tall and lean, a perfect shape for caving. He smiled back at me, eager to get to the task at hand.

I picked up the backpack containing the high-resolution scientific camera and a variety of photographic scales—standard tools for measuring archaeological finds—and tossed it over to him. Sure that Matt could handle the narrowest slot, I had spent the past four days teaching him how to take a properly scaled scientific picture. The entire point of this evening's exercise was to get good, scaled photographs of the hominin fossils, and any other fossils that were in the chamber. The last thing I wanted was to push the button on a major expedition for something I wasn't 100 percent sure about. I also had talked Matt through a strategy to photograph as much of the cave as possible, and to try to identify what fossils were actually there. Having grown up in the fossil business, so to speak, he could do the job I needed done.

As we approached the cave entrance Rick and Steven led us to, I glanced about in the dark, getting my bearings, and tried to remember if I had ever been here before. Only a few hundred meters away was the outline of a hill, with Swartkrans near the crest of the opposite side. I had been there hundreds of times in the past 23 years. A little farther away I could see the lights of the Sterkfontein visitors center. We were right in the heart of the Sterkfontein Valley, the most explored fossil-bearing area on the continent. Standing there, I realized that not only had I been in this area before but in these precise caves, the Rising Star and Empire systems. I had surveyed this farm during the Atlas Project, and not more than 200 meters away was one of the fossil-bearing sites from that expedition.

As we walked up the slight slope of the hill, our headlamps flickering across the uneven ground in front of us, I asked no one in particular questions about the site in advance of entering. "How far in is it?"

"Not too far" was Steven's unhelpful answer.

"How bad are the squeezes?" Squeezes are the narrowest part of a cave passage, where you literally squeeze your way through narrow choke points of rock. They set the limits on who can enter deeper.

"A bit," someone else I couldn't see in the darkness answered.

"And the climbs?" I asked.

"Some," laughed Rick.

"You'll fit," added Pedro, although he chuckled somewhat ominously, too.

I was quickly learning that this group of cavers didn't speak much, or at least tonight they were going to let me find out for myself. Maybe, I thought, there was a reason for this?

We reached the cave entrance and I scanned the narrow opening with my headlamp. To the left was a black void, a drop-off of unknown depth. To the right, a tree obstructed the route in, forcing us to edge closer to the sheer drop-off. Nice.

Just beyond that danger point was a rock archway that was clearly man-made, perhaps by miners blasting an entrance back in the 19th century. The experienced cavers were already starting down ahead of me. Matt eagerly followed. Slipping on my caving gloves, I followed the group down into the darkness.

Thirty minutes later I was having second thoughts. I found myself pressed into a narrow space. A sharp knob of rock pushed painfully into my ribs. My right arm was stretched out in front of me, my left crammed tightly by my side. My whole vision was filled with cave floor, and tilting my neck up a little rewarded me with a clonk of my helmet on the low ceiling of the passage. I could just see a light ahead at the end of the tunnel and Dave peering back at me, grinning.

"Just a bit more!" he said, a little too cheerfully.

I kicked, my feet stretched behind me, trying to get traction on the slippery mud-coated rock. I was wedged tightly in place and could only move forward with little wriggles, exhaling to make my chest smaller, pushing forward, sticking like a cork with each inhale. This was "Superman's Crawl," so named because all but the skinniest cavers had to extend one arm over their head to squeeze through the seven-meter-long passage. With one hand forward, one back by my side, I pushed through, centimeter by centimeter.

A few minutes later, free of the squeeze, I could stand. I brushed some of the wet mud from the front of my overalls, a futile gesture considering the sheer amount of mud and dirt all around. My headlamp's light played about the faces of those around me, and behind me, Rick slipped out of the crawl as if he had walked through standing up. Matthew followed right behind, grinning and clearly loving this.

"How much farther?" I asked.

"A bit," came the helpful answer.

But now I could take a moment to look around on this side of Superman's Crawl. "Fossils," I said, fingering a glistening baboon tooth that protruded from the wall.

"The walls are covered in them," Steven agreed, gesturing to another one on the opposite wall—and indeed they were. This chamber alone deserved further investigation, but we were here to see fossils farther on.

"Do we wait on Pedro and the others?" I asked.

Pedro and a few other cavers who were not "physiologically appropriate" to pass through Superman's Crawl had taken another, longer route, through an area that had a well-known squeeze called "Postbox," because you slipped through it as if you were a letter dropped into a slot.

"No, they'll catch up," answered John as he moved off down a narrow passage. "We have some climbing to do."

Reaching the base of an old roof collapse, Steven leaped nimbly up onto a jagged edge of rock, leading the way. The whole line of rock pushed upward in a series of large scalelike flat rocks that ascended into the darkness above.

"Up there?" I pointed my headlamp upward into a space so vast, the light failed to reach the ceiling.

"Yup, it's called the Dragon's Back," Steve replied, already meters above me and climbing the wet rock quickly.

I looked over at Dave Ingold and asked how deep we were.

"About 40 meters."

Matt, Dave, John, and the others quickly followed Steven's ascent route. Shrugging, I thought, "In for a penny, in for a pound," as I pulled my body up onto the narrow edge of the Dragon's Back and began the climb. Already I saw how difficult mounting an expedition in this cave system would be. The whole journey was dangerous. I guessed that we must already have come a hundred meters to get to this point, though it was hard to assess with all the twists and turns of the passages. Getting any sort of equipment in here would be a nightmare. Caves like this often have loose ceilings, as tree roots can penetrate deep and destabilize the rock as they seek water deeper down. Not to mention—I thought to myself as I glanced down the knife-edged Dragon's Back—a single slip off these rocks, with a fall of what looked to be about a dozen meters or more, might result in serious injury or even death.

The experienced cavers took the Dragon's Back in safe, measured movements, expertly navigating up the sheer, wet rocks. Matthew did the same, but with the fearlessness of youth. I am not ashamed to admit that I took a bit longer to traverse the 17 meters it took to reach the top of the climb.

At last we were at the top, with only one more obstacle to go. Here one had to step across a gap about a meter wide, the drop below going all the way back down to the floor of the cave 15 meters below. I took the leap over the vertical crevasse, joining the others on a small rock ledge.

"This is it," Steven said. I pressed myself against the wall behind me and leaned over so that I could peer around him. I would have to crawl on my belly to go any farther. Getting down on my hands and knees, and then flat on my chest, I wriggled into the tight space that Steven had indicated. Rick slithered ahead of me, squeezing himself into what seemed an impossibly small niche at the end of the passage, making room for my approach.

Rick gestured forward with his toes. "That's it," he said, as I inched my way forward over the sharp rock.

"You're kidding," was my honest response.

Rick was sticking his foot into a vertical slot that looked to be just slightly wider than his boot.

"You're kidding," I repeated, looking at the slot in disbelief.

Wriggling forward a bit more, I pressed my face into the fissure and let the light on my helmet shine down into the darkness, illuminating the vertical shaft below. I didn't think my head would even fit through the narrow opening. Sharp, jagged rocks jutted out into the slot. I looked up at Rick in disbelief, shaking my head in wonder that he and Steven had ever gone down this chute.

"Is this the only way in?" I asked.

A muffled answer, interrupted by grunts, came from somewhere below and behind me. "Looks like it, but we're trying!" Dave and John were looking for a different way into the fossil chamber, but they weren't having any success.

All I could say was "OK" as I squeezed my way backward out of the entrance to make way for the others to get through the slot.

I turned my headlamp off to conserve batteries and maneuvered myself onto the small ledge, trying to find a comfortable position. Matthew, Rick, and Steven had descended, and the other cavers had moved farther away in search of other access routes to the chamber below. Silence soon prevailed as I was left in total darkness to contemplate the way forward.

As I sat alone there in the dark, my mind was spinning. Could this really be the kind of paradigm-shifting find I think it might be?

The last four days had been a whirlwind. After Pedro, Rick, and Steven first showed me the pictures from this chamber, I had sat up late thinking about what the discovery might mean. If these were hominin fossils, as inaccessible as this chamber seemed, they were open and exposed to other cavers who might hear about them. We needed to assess the site quickly and work to establish how best to excavate. I had called Terry Garcia, executive vice president for mission programs at National Geographic, and he had agreed to support the work. But before spending so much effort and funding, I needed a second opinion.

The next day, I sent copies of the photos to colleagues I trusted: John Hawks, Darryl de Ruiter, Steve Churchill, and Peter Schmid. Although the four scientists' opinions varied, all agreed that the fossils represented some kind of primitive hominin, particularly considering the jawbone with its teeth in place. Like me, none of them noted any duplicates among the bones they saw in the photographs. That suggested that the bones might represent a single skeleton—a remarkable find made only a handful of times before, as we all knew. Their observations supported my original impressions, but I needed more than Rick and Steven's amateur photos before launching a major expedition.

So now, in the dark, facing the reality of this site, I started thinking through the logistical challenges that faced me. If the fossils were what we thought they were, this was going to require a large operation. Just the safety protocols that would have to be put in place to do this work would be immense. And who would carry out the work? I needed people with the expertise to excavate precious fossil hominin material, and the skills and mental attitude—and body size—to get down that narrow chute. I could well imagine that conditions in the chamber itself were even more dangerous than where I was sitting. There would be a danger of $CO_2$ buildup, collapse, and injury down there. Now that I was in the cave, I could see that there was potential danger along the whole route into the chamber.

I started thinking about the infrastructure I would need for such an expedition, envisioning something like my fellow National Geographic explorers Bob Ballard and James Cameron had used in their undersea expeditions. A series of hardwired cameras and telephones would keep the scientists underground in contact with the surface. That was going to take a lot of cable. Here we must be something like 200 meters into the cave, taking into account all of the twists and turns. The equipment would also need to be waterproof, or at least water-resistant, to survive for any length of time in this wet environment. Caves can be hostile to sensitive electronics, and so the equipment would have to be extremely durable. In my mind's eye, sitting there alone in the dark, I imagined a command center, with screens and computers, intercoms and other backup communication systems, monitoring and communicating with scientists down below as they excavated the delicate fossils.

Getting fossils out of the chamber was one thing, but that was the final step that could come only after the long scientific process of recording the positions of the fossils in the context where we found them. At Malapa and most other sites, we used laser theodolites—sensitive surveyors' instruments—to record the location of every artifact and bone with an accuracy of millimeters. Here, I doubted that such equipment would even fit down into the chamber, much less be usable within its narrow, twisted confines. But context of finds is everything in our world of paleoanthropology, and so we would have to solve this problem as well.

Finally, after mulling over these problems, my mind went back to what sort of people I could enlist to do this work, and more important, how I was going to find them. Bob Ballard and James Cameron had the luxury of using robots to descend into the deepest parts of the ocean and explore and retrieve artifacts. Paleoanthropology hadn't advanced to that stage yet, so I was going to need skilled—and skinny—humans to work at the end of the communications tether I was designing in my head.

All of this was predicated on the notion that these fossils were those of a primitive human relative. I thought they were, but I had only seen Rick and Steven's first pictures. Crouched there, uncomfortable in the darkness, I could only wait.

❦

Forty-five minutes went by with no sign of Rick, Steven, or Matthew. Occasionally one of the other cavers would come by and chat for a few minutes, before again slipping off to explore. There was still no sign of Pedro. Perhaps he had turned around or found some other part of the system to explore.

A flicker of light came from the narrow shaft. Turning on my own headlamp, I peered eagerly across a meter of space to see who was coming up. With a heave and a grunt, I was relieved to see Matthew haul his shoulders out of the slot. He looked at me, his face smeared with mud but his eyes sparkling brightly. He pushed the backpack that contained the camera toward me as he caught his breath from the climb.

"And?!" I asked impatiently.

"Daddy, it was beautiful!" he said excitedly, "It was so wonderful, my hands were shaking for three minutes before I could take a picture!" He pulled the camera out to show me, smiling as broadly as I have ever seen him smile.

"There's a lot!" he said excitedly as I started scrolling through the pictures on the back of the camera.

The fossils were everything I had thought they might be. Matt had clear pictures of the mandible. He captured a skull embedded partially in the ground and postcranial remains scattered about on the cave floor. All hominin.

"Basically from the moment you drop down into the chamber, all the way to the end, there are pieces of bone lying about all over the floor," he said.

I nodded, excited by what he was saying. Rick, then Steven popped out of the shaft and we all shuffled about, trying to make room to fit together on the ledge.

"What do you think?" asked Rick, looking expectantly at me.

"I think we have a lot of work to do" was my answer.

# 17

The next day, October 6, I sat at my kitchen table looking at the job advertisement I had typed out on my laptop. It was fairly straight-forward, a basic description of the kind of people I would need and the time line for starting work. Working through the morning, I sketched out a plan of the kind of equipment I would need to mount the expedition, created a rough design of the communication systems, drafted a set of safety procedures, and, finally, filled out an application to SAHRA, the South African Heritage Resources Agency, requesting legal permission to do the work.

It had to be a big operation, with all the cavers, scientists, and support people I required, that was for sure. My rough count came up to around 50 people in all. They would have to be housed, fed, and transported. All this had to come together within a three-week period.

Why was I moving so fast? What bothered me most was that I could see from both Steven and Matthew's photos that some of the bones were freshly damaged. As Steven and Rick had assured me again and again, they had been very careful and had not stepped on the material or dislodged any from the cave's floor. That meant other cavers had likely been through that chamber, even though it was not on maps of the site. And then there was that survey marker on the back wall of the chamber. Someone had indeed been in there before, and I had no way of knowing who or when they would be back.

Now, after our trip of last night, perhaps 10 people knew about the existence of important fossils in the chamber. Soon there could be many more.

Though I had warned everyone against it, casual tourism by someone just interested in seeing the material in the chamber, or someone who heard a rumor that it existed, could cause tremendous and irreparable damage. So I was not going to waste any time. I wanted to be in that chamber by November if I could get all the permits and permissions in place and find the right people to do the job.

I needed to get the landowner's permission. Although the cavers knew who that was—a Mr. Leon Jacobs, who had given them permission over the years to cave in the system—they had lost his number. I called a friend, Mags Pillay, at the Cradle of Humankind World Heritage Site Management Authority, informed him of the discovery, and asked for assistance in finding out the landowner's number, the management authority keeping such records. He agreed to help, and offered assistance in fast-tracking permit applications from their side as well.

Now I had to find the right people. I reread my description of the requirements again: knowledgeable scientist, intrepid caver, tiny in stature. Should I just mail this to my colleagues and ask them to distribute it in the normal way? I guessed there probably weren't more than a handful of people in the whole world who fit the description and were available on such short notice. Glancing at my computer screen, I saw a Facebook notification pop up in the corner of the screen. It started me thinking . . . *Why not?*

A minute later, the ad went live. It read like this:

> Dear Colleague—I need the help of the whole community and for you to reach out to as many related professional groups as possible. We need perhaps three or four individuals with excellent archaeological/palaeontological and excavation skills for a short-term project that may kick off as early as November 1, 2013, and last the month if all logistics go as planned. The catch is this—the person must be skinny and preferably small. They must not be claustrophobic, they must be fit, they should have some caving experience; climbing experience would be a bonus. They must be willing to

work in cramped quarters, have a good attitude, and be a team player. Given the highly specialized and perhaps rare nature of what I am looking for, I would be willing to look at an experienced Ph.D. student or a very well trained master's student, even though the more experience, the better (Ph.D.'s and senior scientists most welcome). No age limit here either. I do not think we will have much money available for pay—but we will cover flights, accommodation (though much will be field accom.), food, and of course there will be guaranteed collaboration further up the road. Anyone interested please contact me directly . . . My deadlines on this are extremely tight, so as far as anyone can, spread the word among professional groups.

I sat back and watched the screen. Within minutes I started seeing "shares" and "likes" as social media did its thing. Now I would just have to wait.

The next morning, as I was driving into work, my cell phone rang. It was my assistant, Wilma Lawrence. She sounded unnerved.

"What are you doing?" she asked, her voice a bit tense.

"Why, what's the problem?" I queried, wondering what had got her upset.

"I have a bunch of messages from women giving me their body dimensions!" she said.

I laughed out loud.

"It's OK, Wilma," I reassured her. She must have thought I had put an ad out on a dating site or something.

THE APPLICATIONS CAME ROLLING in. Within a week I had hundreds of inquiries by colleagues and people from around the world. Within 10 days, I had the CVs of almost 60 qualified applicants, the vast majority of them young women. This gender dominance was due in part to the physical requirements: They had to be physically able to fit into the slot, after all. But it also reflected the changing demographics of archaeology and anthropology, in which the strong majority of students and young scientists are now women. The CVs in front of me were impressive as I went through them, ticking off the skill sets one by one. This one had climbing skills, a big plus. This one had emergency medical skills, another plus. As I went through the stack of papers, I was hugely impressed at the varied abilities people had that made them suitable, in a variety of different ways, for this unusual task. I was also humbled by how many people trusted me. I wasn't paying them, after all, and I hadn't even said what we were going to do, yet all these applicants were willing to drop everything and come to South Africa based on that Facebook ad alone.

Short-listing was harder than I thought, but with the assistance of my colleagues, I eventually got the number of applicants down to a dozen highly qualified individuals. I was, by that time, beginning to rethink numbers. Although we were only going in to retrieve a single skeleton, having a few more skilled people to work would mean that we could work longer each day. More scientists would also give us some backup in case of injury.

I set up Skype calls with my top 10 applicants. I decided that even in these first calls, I would begin to test them immediately, because I knew what sort of stresses they would be under. I planned an open communication line into the chamber using a rugged outdoor intercom system, which would let me talk to the excavators at any time without their having to activate the communication system and allow me to hear what was going on as they worked. In other words, it put another virtual excavator into the chamber along with the advance team. So, I decided that I would interview each candidate over Skype, but during the course of the interview, I would cut out the visual communication, and even drop the line as if we had been cut off. I wanted to see how each candidate responded to losing communication in the middle of the interview, how they would deal with changes in the planned scenario—a sort of mini–stress test.

Some applicants fared worse than others. A few simply panicked when I cut the communications. Others sulked audibly. Some had difficulty when

I asked them to describe the room they were sitting in, allowing me to assess their ability to use words to describe things I could not see. To all, I described in great detail just how dangerous and life threatening I felt the operation would be. One of the successful applicants told me later that it was the strangest interview she had ever experienced.

In the end I had eight candidates whom I considered all pretty much equal. I had been brutally honest with each of them. Yes, it was an expedition to recover what we thought was a single hominin skeleton. It was going to be highly dangerous—in fact, if something went extremely wrong, they could be facing a risk of death—but we were taking all precautions to ensure their safety. I emphasized the size of the slot, making sure they understood they needed to squeeze through a gap only 18 centimeters wide. It was going to be tough, dangerous work, and I needed to be sure I could rely on every one of them, and that they could rely upon each other.

I eventually chose six candidates and called each one. My office began making arrangements to fly them out. The next day, two of those candidates backed out. One simply got cold feet, and the other, a young man, told me that he had lied about his measurements. He couldn't fit through such a small gap. I thanked him for his honesty, and though he promised to crash diet, I told him that I just couldn't risk it. Other people's lives were in the balance. I then contacted my seventh and eighth short-listed candidates, who were thrilled.

I had my science team now, who just happened to be all women. Marina Elliott, Lindsay Eaves, Elen Feuerriegel, Alia Gurtov, Hannah Morris, and Becca Peixotto: Each came with her own unique skill set. I chose a diverse team so that their different skills would complement each other, joining a multitude of strengths with few weaknesses.

Tough and wiry, Marina was a Canadian, finishing her Ph.D. in biological anthropology at Simon Fraser University in British Columbia. She was an accomplished forensic anthropologist who had worked in crime labs and morgues and had joined archaeological digs in Siberia and northern Alaska.

Trained as a veterinary technician, she had valuable medical skills, and she carried an impressive set of outdoor skills, including experience as an adventure guide, climber, and caver.

Lindsay was taller and athletic. She came from Texas, having worked on her Ph.D. in paleoanthropology at the University of Iowa. Her CV showed a strong record of excavation skills and a deep knowledge of paleoanthropology. In addition, she had built a good track record as a public communicator of science, something we thought would be of considerable use to our team in the months and perhaps even years ahead.

The only Australian on the science team, Elen, was a thin redhead in the midst of her Ph.D. studies at Australian National University. A student of the well-known paleoanthropologist Colin Groves, she had excellent skills in working with postcranial anatomy, a knowledge base that would be critical underground. Her impressive academic record was supported by extensive experience in caving and climbing.

Petite and dark haired, Alia was a student at the University of Wisconsin and had worked for several years at Olduvai Gorge, Tanzania, trying to understand how the animal teeth from that site could lead to knowledge about the ancient environment. During the interview process, she had tested herself in an MRI machine to prove she could work in tight, claustrophobic spaces. I also anticipated needing her experience with animal bones in the chamber, because the fossil material would inevitably include a large number of animal remains, as always happened in South African sites.

Hannah was tall and slender. She was the softest spoken of the group. Raised in Georgia, my childhood home, she had an excellent record of caving and outdoor experiences, as well as a long history of working on excavations in both historical and archaeological sites and experience handling human remains.

The smallest member of the underground scientific team in physical stature was Becca, but her size belied a toughness and strong background in outdoor skills and leadership. She was an accomplished climber and had been a field instructor for Outward Bound before she moved into archaeological work, exploring for traces of the communities of escaped slaves in the Great Dismal Swamp of southeastern Virginia.

With these six women, we had our core scientific exploration team.

# 18

The team assembled at the site on November 7, a typical springtime Highveld day—bright, sunny, and hot. It had rained the night before, and the air smelled crisp and clean. I arrived on the site with my Jeep fully loaded with supplies. Already, dozens of tents were set up on the campsite in the valley below the hill that held the Rising Star cave system. Peter Schmid and Wayne Crichton had been hard at work setting up the 20 large canvas dome tents that would be our home for the next 21 days. Wayne was a friend of mine who had often walked with me during the surveys back in 2008, and now I hired him as camp manager for the expedition. They had lined up the tents in neat military rows, a combination of Wayne's natural inclination for orderliness and Peter's Swiss heritage, I figured. Others were setting up the three larger tents that would serve as our field kitchen and dining tents.

The previous three weeks had gone by in a blur of activity. Equipment bought, flights scheduled, safety briefings held almost daily. The constraints of the cave had dictated that we needed new types of technology to work in the extreme underground environments. Ashley Kruger, a Ph.D. student of mine and a wizard with technology, had found a new type of handheld white-light scanner that would allow us to do real-time scanning of the ground surface and create high-resolution maps of the fossils where they lay on the cave floor. The scanner, from a company called Artec, would help preserve the entire context of each bone and artifact by creating an accurate three-dimensional image of the site at every step. It was capable of creating images with a resolution of as sharp as 0.1 millimeter of accuracy, better than any used on most archaeological sites. But the Artec scanner was untested in such extreme environments, having been built for medical applications in a clean clinical environment, so the company had sent a technician to the site to assist us. The six scientists who would be carrying out the excavation kept busy training with the device to ensure they could record data quickly and accurately.

As I got out of my vehicle, I stopped for a moment to watch the hive of activity. Near where the kitchen tent would be, its dark green canvas roof laid out on the ground like an enormous picnic blanket, I saw Andrew Howley and John Cullum, Andrew busy typing on his laptop and John fiddling with a camera. Andrew and John were two members of National Geographic's staff who had joined us on the expedition.

In an unusually bold move, National Geographic had agreed to allow our team to take the expedition live on social media, streaming tweets, Facebook posts, and a blog live to the world. All of my colleagues and I were keen on the experiment—a unique chance to recover a fossil hominin skeleton live in front of the world. I asked Andrew and John whether the Rising Star expedition blog had gone live yet and received a thumbs-up from Andrew as I walked by. Later the team would be joined by Garrreth Bird (yes, spelled with three *r*'s), a photographer selected for his underground experience. Garrreth would be the only person besides scientists and safety cavers allowed into the chamber itself. In the distance I could see the PBS *Nova* team setting up a camera to film us setting up camp. By sheer coincidence PBS had been filming a show on Malapa when the Rising Star discovery was made, and with some foresight, had shifted the three-man crew over to this expedition as it unfolded.

Vehicles began to stream onto the scene. I busied myself with unpacking first my kit, then the overalls, safety gear, and odds and ends such as our black baseball caps with "Rising Star" printed in gold and a star sewn in the middle. I checked the quantity, color, and size of each box of overalls.

All duty positions could be identified by the color of the overalls worn—blue for scientists, gray for expert cavers, orange for volunteers, and red for medical personnel—so I could quickly identify who had what role and if they were where they should be.

Steve Churchill walked up to me as I worked on my checklist. "You ready, homie?" he asked, giving me a slap on the back. Like Gladysvale, Palau, and Malapa, this would be another adventure Steve and I were undertaking together.

"As ready as I'll ever be," I answered.

The camp itself was in a pasture that had been chewed down by horses. Across a tiny streambed, a rocky slope leads up to a long hill with a limestone outcropping at the hillcrest. The entrance to the Rising Star cave system is an unassuming dip into that hillside, with a clump of trees blocking the view of it from any distance. It is very different from Gladysvale, with its impressive yawning opening, or Malapa, only a small depression in the ground. But as at those sites, traces of old miners' activity were strewn about, small piles of waste breccia and discarded dolomite. Although the sites of Swartkrans and Sterkfontein both sit within a mile or so of a tarred road, with their impressive breccia deposits clearly visible, Rising Star was a true caver's cave. It held all of its secrets deep belowground.

Over the next three days, the campsite took shape. At the same time, we worked to acclimatize the six advance scientists to the underground environment where they would spend much of the next three weeks. Dave Ingold and John Dickie took them through some tortuous passages, testing their skills, encouraging them, and letting each one gain the confidence she would need to undertake the excavation work and to complete the long journey to and from the Chamber (I had begun to think of it with a capital $C$). Each morning I would work with them on protocols, ensuring that each scientist understood the excavation plan and safety procedures. Every evening Dave and John would brief me on their day's performance underground.

Several of the scientists at first showed anxiety at the tight squeezes, but as they booked more hours underground, they became more comfortable with the challenge. Eventually, Dave and John took them to the top of the Dragon's Back and showed them the Chute, as the slot was now named. One by one, each tested her body's ability to fit by slipping into the top of this narrow squeeze. Each one had to deal with how she would handle the entry and navigate her way down the narrow passageway. Different body shapes required a different series of handholds and footholds. One might wedge her legs to support her weight at one part of the climb, while a shorter or taller climber would find a different way through. Every one of them met with sharp spines of rock, and they developed a routine of checking bumps and bruises after each ascent.

I still had not allowed anyone to set foot into the Chamber. I didn't want to risk the potential of damaging fossils that were lying on the Chamber's floor. But there was much climbing and descending as volunteer cavers as well as our own team worked tirelessly to string almost three and a half kilometers of military-grade video and audio cables all the way to the base of the Chute. Nine cameras were set up along the route and tested: off-the-shelf outdoor security cameras chosen because this technology is rugged and easily replaced. Our team set up LED lights along the route at strategic points, but most of the journey would be lit only by the head-lamps they wore. Each camera also had infrared capabilities in case the lights failed.

I mapped out the critical points where there was the greatest chance of injury. Some were squeeze points where fossils and humans would have to pass; others were places where ropes and ladders would have to be installed. The cavers set up safety ropes along the Dragon's Back. The protocol was that anyone climbing this dangerous part of the route would harness up at the bottom, clip in, and climb. Some of the more daring cavers felt they could handle this climb without ropes, but I insisted on them: safety first. I had promised myself I was not going to lose anyone, and luckily I had the support of John Dickie, who was not an officer of the caving society but also a retired chief petty officer in the navy. We spoke the same language, and he made sure everyone followed the rules rigidly.

One evening as we were preparing for the final dive into the cave, I received an email from the father of one of the advance scientists. He was naturally nervous about his daughter's safety on this expedition, and she had informed him the day before about all of the safety protocols and training they were doing. What touched me was his reason for writing. After hearing from his daughter that I had sent both my son and my daughter down the Chute for safety tests, he wanted to thank me privately. He understood that if I was willing to risk the lives and safety of my own children, then as a parent he was comfortable with entrusting the safety of his daughter with me.

# 19

The setup underground wasn't without snags, and we had to solve a lot of problems on the fly during those first critical days. For instance, our cables could not run by way of the shortest route to the Chamber. Superman's Crawl was so narrow, a person couldn't fit if cables were in there as well. So we rerouted the cables around the longer route, through the Postbox and then up to the top of the Chute. Another problem we encountered was at the base of the Chute. John Dickie and Dave Ingold realized that the last drop, a distance of about two meters, was going to be too much for some of our shorter lead scientists, and so a wooden stepladder had to be constructed at the bottom, each part transported down the Chute by hand. We had a pulley system at the top of the Chute to raise fossils, and this helped in lowering other supplies and equipment down the narrow passage, too.

Next to the entrance of the cave we set up a tent as a Command Center, the communication hub for the whole operation. Just down the hill slope a pair of large tents housed the aboveground science team and the caving gear. The Science Tent would be a practical laboratory for the initial preparation, identification, and cataloging of the fossils as they came out of the cave. The Cavers' Tent would provide a place for cavers and scientists to change in and out of their underground gear, and a shady space to relax.

I sat in the growing Command Center with Ashley, watching him check the computer systems and fiddle with the camera box. The scene began to look more and more like the operation I had first envisioned while sitting alone in the darkness, waiting on Matthew to climb back up from the Chamber back in early October. I glanced up as Pedro walked by with a couple hundred meters of blue video cable slung over his shoulder like a bandolier. He seemed to be having a good time as he disappeared down the cave entrance. Looking about the busy scene, I saw about 50 people at work. Peter Schmid and Steve Churchill were helping secure the Science Tent guide ropes. Others were setting up battery-charging stations. Any long underground expedition quickly uses up batteries, which are your lifeline when you are deep underground and in the dark. So the battery-recharging station was a key operation, with a person singularly responsible for this important task.

I looked at the map in front of me and pictured the path that each of the advance scientists would follow. We had given a name to each point along the route, including each camera position, light position, and communication point. Anyone entering the cave would kit up at the Cavers' Tent, donning her overalls, collecting caving gloves and putting on helmet and light, and ensuring she had a backup light. She would then walk the 30 meters up to the Command Center, where she would clock in, her name and time of entry recorded in the logbook by whomever was on safety duty that day. She would also pick up enough sets of fresh batteries for her predicted time underground, and then an extra set, all checked off by the safety officer. Once this was done, she would remove from around her neck a plastic identity tag—everyone who came onto the site had to wear one of these at all times—and would loop it over a line strung across the entrance of the cave, where the tag would remain until she exited the cave. This line of dangling tags acted as a backup system so that we could tell who was underground at any time. In the case of an emergency, we would know instantly if anyone was still in the cave.

Then the scientists would descend into the darkness of the cave. Ducking their head to enter, they would turn left and enter a narrow passage that immediately began to angle downward. The floor here was slick, because of water dripping from the ceiling, so they had to be careful to avoid slipping onto their backside. Passing this point, they would come to a three-way inter-section and make a sharp turn to the right, descending along an even more narrow passage. Here, pretty much everyone, even the skinniest of our cavers or scientists, had to turn sideways and squeeze between two closely spaced walls of rock. A few dozen meters of these tight squeezes, punctuated by a few short climbs and drops, would bring them to the Ladder. This was the first of our camera positions—a metal ladder that we had roped into the cave. When people were coming up out of the cave, this Ladder-cam gave us a three- or four-minute warning before they appeared at the Command Center.

After the Ladder descent, they would face squeezes and climbs, both up and down, until they reached Superman's Crawl and the second camera. Going down onto their belly, they would begin slithering their way through this narrow seven-meter tunnel. The nimbler, thinner cavers zipped through this, but there would be many humorous moments as slightly larger cavers had their overalls stripped off them within this crawl, caught on camera to the endless amusement of the team manning the Command Center.

Beyond Superman's Crawl the cave opened up a bit, and the scientists could stand again and, if necessary, catch their breath. Here, they would meet the large zip-tied bundle of blue and gray cables coming from a side passage. Following this conduit of cables along a long alley, they would pass another camera at the base of the Dragon's Back. At this point they would be almost 40 meters underground and about 15 minutes into their journey. Here also, they would stop and put on a climbing harness, a set of sewn canvas straps forming loops for both legs and arms. Typically, they would have the assistance of a safety caver positioned at the base of Dragon's Back to help them with this clumsy exercise, attaching a belt around their waist holding a carabiner clip that they hooked into two short safety ropes while they were clipped to a long safety rope affixed to the wall with strong bolts.

Climbing up the imposing rock ridge, the scientists would stop every few meters when they reached a bolt, unfasten one of the short safety ropes, and then clip it to the rope on the opposite side of the bolt. The other short rope would follow. This was to be a slow and deliberate process, to ensure that cavers could never fall more than a few meters if they lost their grip or footing. Even a short fall onto sharp solid rock could cause serious injury, but it's better than falling many meters to the floor below. Once they reached the top of the Dragon's Back, a climb of about 20 meters, they would cross the last meter-wide chasm, still roped in, and arrive at Base 1. Here, wedged between rocks, one or two safety cavers would sit at all times, whenever anyone, scientist or caver, was in the Chamber below. This position at Base 1 was an unenviable one, as the person manning it often had to sit for hours alone in the dark with headlamps off. Aboveground, we would watch their eerie gray image flickering on the screen as they tucked themselves into some cranny to stay comfortable. This assignment quickly picked up a new moniker: Chute Troll.

Upon reaching Base 1, the attending caver was expected to call up to the Command Center. The person manning the desk would log in the time of safe arrival of the scientist. Here was a key safety check: Only one person could be going up or down the Chute at any time, so permission was coordinated from the Command Center. I had written very precise language for each clearance point so there could never be any misunderstanding about a person's permission to descend or whether they should hold at Base 1 for some safety reason. "Thanks, Base 1. You are go for descent." The start of the descent would be recorded into the log at the Command Center desk.

The bottom of the Chute was known as the Landing Zone. Once down, the scientist would lift the receiver, triggering its direct-wired counterpart to ring back in the Command Center. There were three phones on the Command Center desk, one dedicated to Base 1, one to the Landing Zone at the bottom of the Chute, and one for the excavators in the Chamber itself. I would stare at that second phone many hundreds of times over the next several weeks, waiting for the call telling me that the climber had safely made it to the bottom. Typically, the descent within the Chute, about 12 meters down, would take a skilled climber around four minutes. This may not seem like a long time, but imagine taking only 12 long steps over a four-minute period, counting 20 seconds between each step, and you will get an idea just how painstaking this descent is. Going up against the force of gravity is even harder.

Once in the Landing Zone and checked into the Command Center, a safety caver—usually Rick, Steven, or another trusted experienced caver— would assist the scientist in taking off her boots. We adopted a barefoot protocol in the Chamber to ensure that those there could feel anything under their feet. Someone was always positioned in the Landing Zone, but that is as far as he or she could go. Only lead scientists moved beyond this point into the Chamber.

At least that's how everything should work, I thought, as I finished tracing this long route with my fingers. I knew the whole journey would take them about 30 minutes each way. That's a long time to cover such a short distance, and any number of things could go wrong along the way. The thousands of little things that had been planned to bring the excavation to this point, though, were almost all ready. We would do final safety and equipment checks and go over, yet again, the protocols for excavation and emergencies, and then we would be ready to go. The next day, November 9, would be the last day to handle any details, big or little. The first scientists would go into the Chamber sometime on the morning of the 10th if all went as planned.

But who would that be? I had six eager, excellent lead scientists to choose from, each one with a different skill set. Chatting with Steve and Peter that evening over a cold beer, we talked about each of the lead scientists, their differing abilities, strengths, and weaknesses. Finally, we came to a consensus of who the first two would be. I would inform the group the following day.

# 20

I'm an early riser, and each morning I would get up at the Rising Star site just before dawn. Usually Marina Elliott was also up, getting a bite in the kitchen area. I would pull out my whiteboard and begin to outline the briefing for the day, to be held every morning at 6:30—first, the goals for the day; second, the teams and their composition; third and last, the safety protocols and safety reminders. Because most of the people in camp were young and highly attuned to social media, I started naming each day with a hashtag at the top of the briefing board. This became a fun part of our daily ritual.

It was November 9, and tomorrow would be #Hday—Hominid day—the first time scientists would enter the Chamber and recover fossils. Today was the last day to check all systems, making sure the complex camera system worked and we had dotted all of the *i*'s and crossed all of the *t*'s. The day progressed smoothly, and by midafternoon I was confident that tomorrow would indeed be the day of first entry. I called the whole group together. After congratulating everyone—it had been a monumental effort in the short three weeks since this expedition had been conceived to get it designed and now delivered—I got down to the point of the meeting. I announced that Marina and Becca would be the first to enter the system the following morning. I was pleased to see that there were no signs of jealousy among the other lead scientists. Although I am sure there may have been some disappointment, they knew they would all get their chances in the Chamber. I let everyone have an early afternoon off to prepare themselves mentally for the next day. People drifted away to start a small bonfire, listen to music, or shower in one of our outdoor showers before the sun set.

That day John Hawks arrived after sunset. Straight off a long flight from his home in Wisconsin, he was clearly tired but ever ebullient. As I watched by the light of the campfire, Marina—having taken on a clear leadership role in the camp and organization—showed him to his tent. He wandered over to the fire, looking around at all the unfamiliar faces.

"Welcome. I see they've set you up properly," I said as he sat down in one of the canvas chairs around the fire.

"Sure, thanks. This is quite a little city you have going here." He gestured into the darkness.

"You have no idea," I said to John. "It's been a busy few days, but you're just in time. Tomorrow we're going to get some hominin fossils!"

As the sun rose on November 10, the side of my tent glowed and the heat started building inside. The hot sun made oversleeping at this campsite its own punishment, and I rarely had trouble getting everyone up at daybreak. I started the gasoline generator a minute or so after six, and people soon began wandering toward the mess tent, knowing that instant coffee would be ready before too long.

I gave the usual 6:30 briefing, with an estimated time line on first entry. After sending everyone off to do last-minute preparations, I pulled the lead scientists aside and again went through the protocols. Rick and Steven would lead them into the cave. Rick would act as Chute Troll, manning Base 1, and Steve would descend to the Landing Zone, where he would act as safety officer. Matthew, my son, would lead Marina and Becca into the Chamber and point out where the most vulnerable bones were, including the skull. He would then exit.

The plan was first to place marker pins for the Artec scanner. These would be critical for linking scans in the future and needed to be affixed perma-

*"Quite a little city you have going here," John Hawks commented
as he first arrived at the compound quickly established to accommodate
the Rising Star expedition. From this campsite, teams descended
into the cave, sending back video records of what they saw
and ultimately bringing fossils up for further study.*

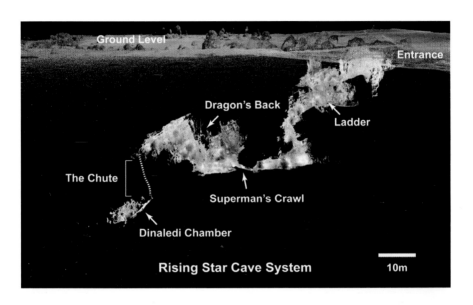

*Members of the expedition had to navigate a complex and tortuous passageway through the Rising Star cave system to reach the Dinaledi Chamber, where the* Homo naledi *fossil trove was found. This cross section image, representing the entire path, is based on laser survey data collected from inside the cave.*

*Avid cavers first told Lee Berger that this inconspicuous opening in the rocky landscape might lead to something of interest. Little did they know that they had found the entrance to a cave full of fossil remains from a species never before identified.*

*Sunlight streams in through the entrance of the Rising Star cave system on anthropologist Marina Elliott, one of the six "underground astronauts" selected to explore the site—all academically and physiologically up to the task, and, by chance, all women.*

*The expedition put team members through many a tight squeeze.
Here Lee Berger emerges from Superman's Crawl, so named because one had
to stretch hands forward, feet back to make it through the space. For many team
members, including Berger himself, the size of their bodies meant they could
never descend all the way into the Dinaledi Chamber.*

*Megan Berger, above, takes up her station at Base 1, at the top of the Chute, as Rick Hunter reaches that point, emerging from the Chamber below.*

*As researcher Marina Elliott, left, collects data about the cave and its contents, teammate Ashley Kruger records her findings on a laptop. Throughout the cave system, electronics including computers, cameras, and spotlights allowed observations to be recorded and transmitted to those outside the cave.*

*Researchers worked in twos and threes once they descended into the Chamber. Here Marina Elliott, left, and Becca Peixotto carefully observe, describe, collect, and catalog fossil specimens found inside the Dinaledi Chamber, more than 100 feet underground.*

*The tension is tangible as a crowd in the Dinaledi Command Center awaits scanned images sent by team members from deep underground.*
*Seated, left to right: Lee Berger, Marina Elliott, and Ashley Kruger.*
*Standing, left to right: Lindsay Eaves, Alia Gurtov, Bonita de Klerk, Gerrie Pretorius, Michael Wall, Matthew Berger, and Steven Tucker.*

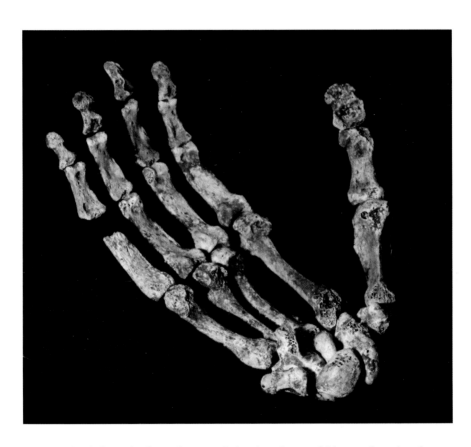

*Once fossils brought from the Dinaledi Chamber could be combined to form
a full hand, the anatomical relationships were striking and distinctive. The long
opposable thumb in particular indicated that the remains were hominin.*

*With hands that show how paleoanthropology can be dirty work, Peter Schmid brushes sediment off one of the teeth discovered in the Dinaledi Chamber.*

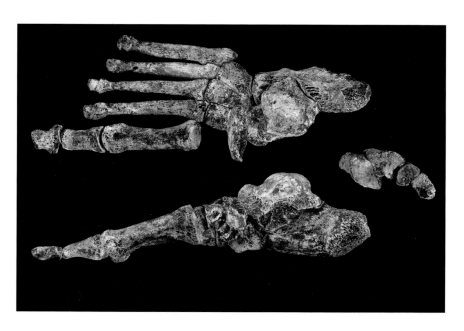

*Among the fossil bones discovered in the Dinaledi Chamber
was a nearly complete right foot, shown here from three different angles:
looking from above, from the side, and, at right, at the near ends
of the five metatarsals, showing the arch of the foot.*

*Rising Star expedition team members divided into groups to focus on different parts of the body. Here members of the cranial team—left to right, Myra Laird, Jill Scott, Heather Garvin, and Davorka Radovčić—compare* Homo naledi *fossils with specimens from other hominins.*

*Rising Star workshop team members set up stations inside the Phillip Tobias Primate and Hominid Fossil Laboratory at the University of the Witwatersrand, where discoveries from nearly a century of South African paleoanthropology are archived in the deep shelves that line three walls.*

*One grand moment of the research came as team members spent several hours laying all the Rising Star fossils out to show the enormous breadth of evidence from across the entire* Homo naledi *skeleton.*

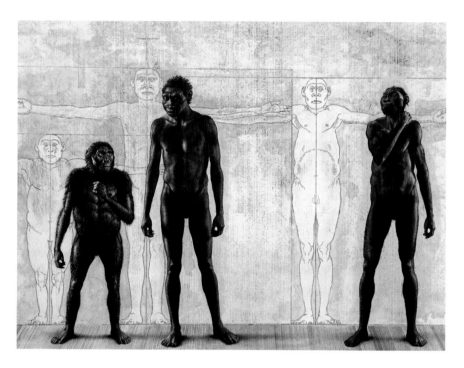

Homo naledi, *shown at right in this artist's interpretation, was the size of a small-bodied human today, making this species taller, with a more slender build, than* Lucy (Australopithecus afarensis), *left, but smaller than the* Turkana Boy (Homo erectus), *center. Many signs point to the Rising Star fossils representing a hominin species never seen before.*

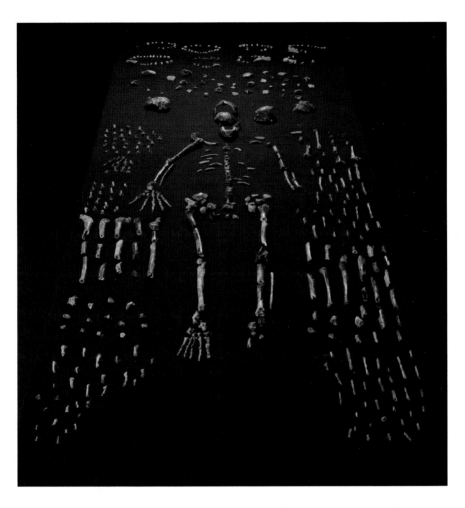

*Arranged to display the best of the entire collection brought up from the Dinaledi Chamber, here the most complete fossils found surround a composite skeleton of* Homo naledi.

*How might these hominin remains have come to be in such a hard-to-reach underground setting? Perhaps, as represented in this imagined scene,* Homo naledi *deliberately brought their dead into the cave—a hypothesis with resounding implications for the story of humankind.*

nently. For markers, we were using simple stainless steel dog tags with personal identification numbers engraved onto them. They would be nailed to the wall as a permanent record of the scanner points. After these were in place, the Chamber floor would be scanned in the vicinity of the first intended excavation area. Only then could collection begin. The first specimen I wanted out was the hominin mandible that we had seen in the photos. It was in a vulnerable position, lying loose on the surface, and of course we all wanted to see it firsthand! Among all the specimens that we could see in the photos, this was the most likely to indicate what species of hominin these remains might represent. The sooner it was out, the sooner we would know a lot more.

My family arrived later that morning to watch the first entry. Megan and Jackie took up residence in the Command Center as Matthew tried on his caving gear. I walked up the hill to give a last interview for the National Geographic blog site before this first cave entry. During the middle of the interview, Andrew Howley asked me how I would describe the lead scientists. I immediately answered, "They're like astronauts, but underground astronauts!" I had grown to think of them in just that way. With their blue jumpsuits and their willingness to risk their lives to recover fossils, I felt then, and still do, that they were every bit as heroic as space travelers. So Andrew started calling them the Underground Astronauts in his blog—and the nickname stuck.

It turned out we were not ready as planned for the cave entry by late morning. As lunchtime and then early afternoon crept away, I worried whether we would get into the cave at all that day. We kept bumping into glitches, particularly with the all-important camera system. But by midafternoon, everything came together. I looked around at the large group in the Command Center and announced, "It's a go!"

There were cheers and backslapping and a few hugs, and then everyone moved off to prepare for the first descent into the Chamber.

Marina and Becca, led by Matthew and Steven, would be the first scientists into the Chamber. As they nervously stood by the cave entrance, completely kitted out, I gave each of them a hug, and then I smiled, trying to exude confidence. They knew their jobs; we had prepared as much as we could. I looked at each of them.

"Ready?"

"As ready as we'll ever be," quipped Marina. Becca simply grinned and nodded.

"Happy hunting!" I said as I gave my son another hug, shook Steven's and Rick's hands, and sent them down into the cave with a pat on the back.

All work came to a standstill as people crowded around the outside of the Command Center. John and Ashley had set up extra monitors so people could watch what was on the screens. The interior of the Command Center was usually off-limits to anyone unauthorized, as the safety of the scientists and cavers depended on there being few distractions, but this first time would be something of an exception as people stayed outside the tent, watching the infrared images of five people descending into the darkness.

"They're at the Ladder," I noted aloud, tapping the screen as we watched them carefully descend, one by one.

"They're through Superman's Crawl." Given the physiques of these five, this squeeze was no obstacle, and they slipped through in minutes.

We all watched silently, though, as they each climbed the Dragon's Back, a much slower process with the safety harnesses and gear in place. After almost 15 minutes, Rick, the last person in line, passed the camera at the top of Dragon's Back and gave a little wave, which caused a chuckle to pass among the tense crowd surrounding and within the Command Center.

A few minutes later, the phone gave its distinctive buzz and I picked it up to hear Steven on the other end of the line: "We're at Base 1."

I answered back, "Thanks, Base 1. You are go for descent."

I entered the start time of Steven's climb into the log. Everyone's eyes were glued to the screens as we watched Steven maneuver himself into the narrow slot and then vanish from our sight. As Matthew moved into view of the camera and positioned himself near the phone, I caught myself biting my lower lip with tension. Was it really worth it to risk people's lives, even my own son's, for fossils? But it was a bit late for self-doubt.

The second phone buzzed a few minutes later: "This is Steve. I'm at the Landing Zone."

"Copy that, Steve. Stand by. We'll send Matthew down." I picked up the Base 1 phone.

"Base 1, this is Command Center. Steve is down safely; Matthew can start his descent."

Matthew's safe arrival five minutes later was followed by a call for Marina to descend. The tension was palpable in the tent. This was the first untested person to descend into the Chamber, and the first scientist in history to enter. We waited as the minutes went by. Four, then five, then six minutes. She was taking longer than either Steven or Matthew. I glanced over at John, who stood opposite me, taking pictures of the scene. I raised my eyebrows at him, and he simply gave me a reassuring smile in return. There was more silence, and then the Landing Zone phone sounded. I picked it up and heard Marina's voice on the other end.

"This is Marina. I'm at the Landing Zone." A cheer erupted around the tent as people high-fived her safe arrival.

I gave the go-ahead for Becca, and she quickly disappeared down the slot, leaving Rick sitting alone at Base 1. Again we waited silently as four, then five minutes passed. Once again, the Landing Zone phone buzzed. I picked it up, listened for a moment, and then put the phone down and said, "Becca's safely down!" Again the tent erupted with cheers.

It felt like a real accomplishment just to get the archaeologists into the Chamber safely. Now they could employ the excavation protocols we had all worked so hard on. Matthew took about half an hour to show Marina and Becca where the fossils were located, and where to step to avoid damaging others on the floor, and then he began his ascent up the Chute, leaving the three-person team behind.

Marina and Becca began to acclimate themselves to the Chamber. As Marina later recounted, it was so silent there, footsteps and fabric noise were the only thing they could hear as they looked around them. The floor of the Landing Zone sloped steeply from the rear wall of the cave for a few meters, until the point where the walls closed into a narrow passage split by a sheet of rock. Still sloping, the Chamber opened up again into a wider area two or three meters across. Although the ceiling of the Chamber was low in the Landing Zone, here it opened upward into a tall Gothic-like arch, nearly 10 meters above the floor. The floor itself was a very finely textured cave earth— the wet brown dust that had lain there for eons.

Here, more than 30 meters below the surface of the earth, we were about to find the bones of an extinct hominin.

# 21

The bones that littered the floor were coated in brown clay that stuck to their surfaces. Here and there, white flecks shone on the cave floor, indicating that some of these bones had been broken, not long ago. This damage, almost certainly from some caver who apparently did not notice the significance of what he passed, had prompted the urgency of this expedition. Large blocks of dolomite bedrock thrust up out of the clay, some with bones atop them. I knew they were the ones Steven and Rick had placed there to photograph on that second visit.

I waited long enough for Marina and Becca to enter the end of the Chamber and then tested the intercom system, using the third phone set up solely for this purpose. My voice should come over the speaker Rick and Steven had set up earlier in the Chamber. We had no visuals yet: Marina and Becca still had to connect the two final cameras.

"How's it looking down there?" I asked. I could hear the echo of my voice in the Chamber.

"It's all good!" replied Becca.

"All good," agreed Marina, although I could tell that they were preoccupied with the setup and the tension of having just arrived.

Soon one of the blank blue screens, the one labeled "Camera 6," flickered to life, resolving a hazy image into the face of Marina, peering into the lens. I picked up the phone.

"We've got you on Camera 6," I said.

"OK!" She smiled into the lens.

Becca and Marina began to unpack and set up the other equipment. Their mission was to scan the cave and recover the mandible as the first find. We watched them set up the laptop computer and connect the Artec scanner. As they activated it, a fluorescent tube cast a bright white light, and the scanner began capturing data, rhythmically flashing as it started in on the essential work of mapping all the specimens. If the scanner failed, we would have to stop the entire excavation until we figured out another mapping solution. The flickering image of the cameras made many of us feel as if we were witnessing a space walk. We watched in tense silence from the surface above them, unable to participate or help.

EVERY ARCHAEOLOGICAL DISCOVERY IS an act of destruction. The debris of thousands of years sits locked within sediments, the position of every artifact and bone holding clues about how they are related to each other and to the creatures who may have left them there. Digging into such a site necessarily destroys this arrangement, and if archaeologists do not record exact details before excavating, critical information will be lost forever. This is one reason it is responsible to leave some parts of archaeological sites in place without digging them, in case some future technology will be able to recover information that we cannot obtain today.

At a site in the open air, or even in many caves, researchers can stretch a large grid of string across the entire area, measuring distances in vertical depth from the gridlines, pinpointing the three-dimensional locations of objects that way. Because the area we were exploring was such a small space, a grid like that was impossible: It would completely impede movement and create risks for the artifacts and the explorers. It was a problem we hoped the scanner would solve. By scanning the entire surface of the Chamber into the computer, we could record the three-dimensional position of everything. Following excavation protocol, the team was to catalog bone fragments and samples, scan the entire surface, and only then lift the artifacts. This tech-

nique allowed us to virtually re-create the entire three-dimensional configuration of the site as if we had virtual x-ray vision and could take the site
apart bone by bone and put it back together again.

The first scan took a long time. Eventually, though, the whole area around
the mandible was scanned. I breathed a sigh of relief: The system was working
so far. We all watched as Marina cataloged the area and prepared the label
that would accompany it from here forward. Becca started up the scanner
again, slowly sweeping it across the cave surface as if she were spray-painting
it. As she did so, a virtual model of the surface appeared on the laptop screen,
now without the mandible in place—a virtual before-and-after picture in
three dimensions had thus been captured.

Then something started beeping: the carbon dioxide detector. Carbon
dioxide buildup is one of the very real dangers of working in limestone cave
systems. Heavier than air and odorless, it can build up to dangerous levels
in confined spaces with poor airflow. It can also build up as a simple factor
of exhalation in relatively sealed chambers. At low levels it's harmless, but
once it rises above one percent in the atmosphere—a situation cavers call
"foul air"—it can be incredibly dangerous. The effects are first rapid breath-
ing and increased heart rate, but carbon dioxide poisoning can quickly lead
to loss of consciousness and even death.

Marina called up on the telephone. "Command Center, we have a carbon
dioxide alarm."

"OK, copy that. Let's get you guys up now." We had rehearsed for just
such an event, and Marina, Becca, and Steven calmly closed down the work
they were doing and ascended, retracing their route back out of the cave
with no incidents. As we all looked on anxiously from the surface, their
images appeared on each of the cameras in reverse order, every few minutes
reaching a new checkpoint until they were at the Ladder. Then, five minutes
later, they emerged from the cave.

They had been underground an hour and a half in total. Despite the scare
of the carbon dioxide alarm, both Marina and Becca were beaming as they
came out of the cave, dirt smudged onto almost every surface of their blue

jumpsuits and faces. We all applauded, and I couldn't help giving each a hug, relieved they were out safely. I was surprised to see that Becca had along with her the gray watertight bag meant for bringing fossils up from the Chamber. She handed it to me with a smile.

"You collected the mandible?" I asked.

"Of course," she responded.

I was thrilled.

Carrying the bag down the hill to the Science Tent, I felt like the Pied Piper of Hamelin, with a trail of cavers, scientists, and students following me. I handed it over to Steve Churchill, with Peter Schmid hovering next to him, and watched as Steve carefully unwound the bubble wrap and exposed the jawbone. People crowded around. I looked over Steve's shoulder at one of the most wonderful sights I had ever seen: the right half of a fossil hominin mandible.

It was broken at the front, just at the level of the fourth premolar, and the joint that attaches the jaw to the skull was broken off the back of it. A hard coating of brown clay clung to one side, but otherwise the jaw was pristine, the enamel of its teeth shiny and bright. First Steve, then Peter examined it for a few moments. Then I handled the specimen myself.

I lifted the small jaw for the first time. I was surprised at how light it was. In many of the fossils from other sites of the Cradle, the original substance of the bone has been replaced almost entirely by hard calcite, making them dense and heavy. Many of the *sediba* fossils, for example, have been partially transformed to stone in this way. But some fossils remain light, having lost some of their mineral content. This fossil jaw was very light: It felt fragile.

*The first jawbone recovered from Rising Star*

I examined the specimen, turning it over in my palm. I was shocked. It was smaller than any of us had expected from the photos. The proportions were what the photos had led us to expect: The third molars were the largest teeth, as in australopiths and different from humans. But the teeth were tiny, really no larger than those of a modern human. I had never seen teeth so small in any extinct hominin. I passed the mandible to John Hawks to have a look and leaned back, not really listening to all the excited voices around me, just thinking: What was this creature?

MEANWHILE, THE HARD DRIVE with the scan data had gone up to the Command Center, where Ashley Kruger had gone to work. Ashley was responsible for managing the data generated by the underground scanner. As he loaded up the data from the hard drive, a ghostly pink landscape appeared on the computer, the three-dimensional surface model of the floor of the Chamber. The crowd moved back to the Command Center to watch this activity. It was, I thought to myself, like watching a crowd at a golf tournament moving from one hole to another, unsure of which famous pro to follow. Everything was interesting now that the science of the expedition had begun. The images coming from the scanner were stunning as Ashley worked on them. Later, he would overlay the data with the color images from the scanner to create a virtual model of the surface just as the excavation team had seen it.

As it turned out, the carbon dioxide scare had been a false alarm. The detector had been mistakenly set to sound the alarm at the slightest elevation in $CO_2$. That was a big relief. After recalibrating, we never heard a further peep from it. As deep as the Chamber was underground, enough air flowed through the cracks and narrow passageways to keep the $CO_2$ levels safe.

As sunset approached, the video feed caught a handful of bats winging up past the Ladder. The team was outside, posing for pictures, and then time for supper. We turned off the generator and called it a night.

# 22

The real work began on Monday. Marina and Becca had seen in person what the photos and video from the cave clearly showed: Bones were strewn across large parts of the Chamber floor. Several of the long bones looked hominin, they were certain. It was time to recover them. Four more archaeologists were eagerly waiting for their turn.

The morning work began with Alia and Elen descending into the cave. The first task in the Chamber itself was to clear all the bones that were on the surface. This required scanning the surface first, then collecting the elements one by one. The first bag of fossils brought to the surface that morning, to our wonder, held only hominin bones, including a beautiful right proximal femur (the top of a thighbone) and a first metacarpal (thumb bone). These were crucial finds.

The femur was similar to those found in australopiths like *africanus* and *afarensis,* with a long neck and small head. Modern human femoral necks, and those few from *Homo erectus,* tended to be short, stout, and rounded in cross section. This one, oval in cross section, didn't look very human.

The first metacarpal was just as fascinating. This is the bone in the palm of the hand that connects to the base of the thumb. Peter brought it to me from the Science Tent. "I've never seen anything like this," he said, holding it out in the palm of his hand.

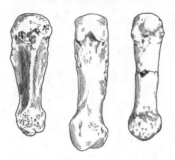

*Left to right, a first metacarpal from Rising Star, from a chimpanzee,
and from Malapa's A. sediba*

I picked it up, turning it over. Neither had I. In a modern human, the first metacarpal is a small bone that looks a lot like a cartoon dog bone: a stick with two identical fatter ends. But this one was narrow at the wrist and wide where the thumb attaches. I shook my head and said, "It's long, though." The length of that bone in the palm of the hand reflects the length of the thumb, and a long opposable thumb was a sure sign of a hominin.

Peter nodded in agreement, though I could tell he was puzzled, too. "It doesn't look like anything I have ever seen," he repeated. Coming from Peter, this was saying quite a lot. Few people alive had dissected more apes and humans than Peter, who came from a long line of classical comparative anatomists in Zurich. He had also seen practically the entire hominin record in his more than 50 years in the field. If he hadn't seen anything like this thumb bone, it truly was unusual.

I went back to the Command Center. It was time for Lindsay and Hannah to make their first trip into the Chamber. I sent a student to find them and tell them to kit up.

The next bag containing fossils that came up brought Steve Churchill from the Science Tent to the Command Center. "You're going to want to see this," he said with a grin.

It was another femur, also from the right side. We had a second individual! By that afternoon, a third right femur came up—yet another individual. Just this one day's work had produced a healthy collection of around 40 individual hominin remains. Although that may not sound like many to most people, I knew this was one of the richest hauls of hominins in a single day of discovery ever. It had taken us months to collect such a number from Malapa, and Malapa had been one of the richest fossil hominin sites in history. From nearby Sterkfontein, a sum total of just over 700 individual remains had been collected, but that was from almost 70 years of nearly continuous work. The number of fossil hominin remains we had found in one day was simply unprecedented, and the mood in the camp was buoyant.

We had also found four bird bones, all lying on the surface. It appeared as if an owl had somehow got into the Chamber and died a long time ago, but long after the fossil hominin remains had been deposited there. Other than those four bones, everything that had come up so far was hominin. At the time, I attributed this just to chance. I was sure we would start to see more animal remains the next day.

That afternoon, as I was closing up the Command Center, Steven Tucker and Rick pulled me aside. They looked serious.

"What's up?" I asked.

Steven looked at Rick, then back to me. "You know, after seeing that femur today—" he started. Rick interrupted—"we think we found another one just like it."

I looked at them both. "Where?" I asked, presuming it was somewhere in the Chamber.

"In a completely different part of the cave system," Rick replied. "Do you want us to go get it?"

I thought about this for a moment. I admit I was tempted. Another hominin find would be great, but I had an entire team focused on the work at hand. If indeed Rick and Steven had found another hominin site, fantastic, but we already had a dangerous job at hand. I made a snap decision.

"Don't mention it to anyone," I said. "I don't want them distracted. If we finish this job, you can go after this next one."

Both of them nodded, though I could see they were as eager as fox terriers to go fetch this bone. I grinned as I watched them walk off. More? Was that possible?

# 23

On Tuesday morning, I wrote on the briefing board: "#SkullDay." I had seen the skull in the original photos. It appeared as a faint circular outline of white material shining in contrast with the brown cave floor. Most of the bones we could see in the original photos seemed to be lying loose upon the surface, but the skull was embedded in the soil of the cave floor. The previous day's finds of multiple skeletons in the cave had surprised us. Now we all wondered: What could lie beneath the surface?

By that time, we had seen enough of the fragile condition of the bone coming out of the cave to know that skull removal would be a delicate operation. We decided to work three team members at a time in the Chamber. One team member would scan and collect from the surface while the two others would slowly work around the skull with paintbrushes, gently removing teaspoons of sediment to be bagged and sent up to the Science Tent. Here scientists and students would work through it again with brushes, looking for tiny fragments of bone. I had decided as part of the protocol we would keep every ounce of sediment from the excavation—a procedure that later proved invaluable.

After an hour, the team had cleared enough sediment to show that the skull was not alone. It rested atop of a tangle of long bones. For another two hours we watched the excavation on the video monitors. Gradually, bit by bit, the edges of each bone came into view as team members patiently continued their work.

A big storm was brewing on the eastern horizon, and I called down on the intercom to pull out the team. With the potential of lightning, we needed to shut down all the sensitive electronics on the surface. The team started up right away.

The storm hit before they could get up, and it was a doozy. The region around the Cradle of Humankind has one of the highest lightning strike rates in the world, and it seemed like it was trying to prove that statistic to us with this storm alone. With people running frantically about, trying to secure guide wires and wildly flapping tent flaps, I spent my time trying to keep the Command Center from blowing away, while still keeping an eye on the screens and watching the progress of the scientists and cavers coming out of the cave. Once I saw they had reached the Ladder, I instructed Ashley to shut down the systems and I raced down to the Science Tent to see if I could help secure things. Entering the tent amid loud crashes of thunder, I found John Hawks literally holding the large tent down by bracing the center pole. I cringed: He was effectively embracing a lightning rod.

"That's probably a bad idea!" I shouted out above the storm.

John's eyes went wide, and he let go quickly. That was dedication to saving fossils, for sure!

✣

THE STORM PASSED AS quickly as it had arrived, with no serious damage left behind. That evening the more senior scientists sat with the underground astronauts to hear about the excavation of the skull.

"It's a puzzle box," Elen told us. "You know that toy where you have to remove one little piece at a time, all in exactly the right order, and you can't tell them apart? That's what this is. A puzzle box." It was a good description of the complex network of bones that surrounded the skull. Every brush-stroke revealed another bone. The floor, it seemed, was literally composed of bones—and so far they all were hominin.

Day two moved on to day three as the underground astronauts, runners, Chute Trolls, and safety cavers smoothly rotated through the Chamber in shifts of four or five hours. The recovery of the skull was taking more time than I had planned because of the complexity of the Puzzle Box, as we now called it. Whenever an excavator uncovered a new piece of long bone beneath the skull, she had to follow its length to figure out how it lay and where it ended. Often the fragment lay under yet another bone. Slowly, painstakingly, the work moved outward one teaspoonful at a time. What started as a small excavation radius just around the skull kept growing until it was an area nearly 18 inches across. All along, the team was collecting more and more bones from this little plot.

Meanwhile, team members aboveground in the Science Tent had developed a routine for preparing and cataloging the fossils and storing them in our on-site safe. I spent most of my time monitoring the video cameras and giving advice to the excavators when they called up with questions. Our carefully planned systems seemed to be working.

Something was bothering me, though. Other than those few bird bones, not a single bit of fauna had come up from the Chamber. At first it had occurred to me that in their enthusiasm to find hominin fossils, the six excavators might have been collecting those first and leaving other animal bones in place. But now we had dozens and dozens of individual fossils. If they were indeed leaving other types of bones behind, they needed to start bringing everything up.

At the end of her afternoon shift, I pulled Marina aside. She was tired and dirty, but she was clearly enjoying herself. After asking her some general questions, I got around to what had been bothering me. "Are all of you cherry-picking only hominin remains?"

"No," she said, surprised at my question. "That's all there is."

✣

THAT EVENING I ASKED Peter, Steve, and John to drive down the road with me to a local pub. As we sat down with a cold one, I voiced what I suspected all of us were thinking.

"What the hell are we dealing with here?" I asked them. "I've never seen anything like this. That Chamber is full of only hominin bodies."

"I don't understand it. Where are the fauna?" Peter agreed, shaking his head as he took a sip of beer.

"Look," John said, "the bones are not chewed. We've got a good number of hand and foot bones, complete, and that's funny too. We don't seem to be missing body parts."

"And I haven't seen any carnivore damage," Steve added. Peter nodded in agreement.

The lack of any signs of carnivore damage was striking. Predators and scavengers play a role in accumulating bones at most cave sites. The bones collected by these animals are leftovers of meals, and they have bite and chew marks, signatures of the culprit that created the assemblage. These fossils had none of those signs.

We all looked at each other, thinking the same thing.

Though the four of us had different backgrounds, we each had significant experience working at archaeological or paleontological excavations. At some point we had all worked around human burials; we had all been broadly trained in forensics. We knew that, typically, in South African cave sites the vast majority of what we find are nonhuman animals. Carnivores of many varieties, antelopes, other animals like giraffes or zebras, even rodents, birds, and lizards—we call them all fauna. In almost every fossil situation, fauna represent the vast majority of any bone assemblage.

Hominin fossils, on the other hand, are extremely rare. Roughly tens of thousands, if not hundreds of thousands, of faunal remains are found for every single hominin fossil. This situation is the same in the Rift Valley of East Africa, and in practically every other natural collection situation in the world. Malapa had been an exceptionally rich hominin site, but still the fauna vastly outnumbered the hominin skeletons.

Beyond that, fossil groupings of a single species of animals—what we call a monospecific assemblage—are extraordinarily rare in the fossil record. Usually, when a monospecific assemblage is found, it is the scene of some easily identifiable catastrophic event, like a flood or mass kill site. But even these situations usually include some other species of animals. When a natural catchment traps animals, it usually traps other things too. If a herd of wildebeests drowned in a river, for example, a paleontologist will also find fish fossils, crocodile teeth, and bits of bone that would normally be in the gravel of a river. Maybe even some zebras amid the herd.

One animal is an exception to this rule, and that's modern humans. Humans are commonly found as monospecific assemblages because we collect our dead and place them together deliberately, keeping them away from other animals. It's a completely unnatural behavior for other animal species, but it's a defining character of many human cultures: deliberate body disposal.

This site was getting stranger and stranger.

# 24

Four days later, the excavation team was still working on that skull. We had established a work pattern, with two or three excavators in the cave before seven o'clock each morning, a changeover during the late morning, and the last crew coming out of the cave sometime around three o'clock in the afternoon. Despite our high hopes, the work on the skull had stretched on much longer than we had expected. Day after day began with the same word on the briefing board: #Skull.

Friday, though, it looked as if it was really going to happen. The team underground had exposed enough area around the skull that we could begin to understand how the deposit was put together—and bring up the skull.

We were facing an unexpected problem. The fossils were building up quickly, and the Science Tent was running out of room. Most of the bones were extremely well preserved—among the best I had seen at any fossil site. But they were damp, and we needed to allow them to dry very slowly and naturally. If their outer and inner layers dried at different rates, the bones might crack. But this took a lot of space, and space was hard to come by. "There's another safe," I mentioned.

"We already filled it," someone replied. My eyes goggled.

We had solved another problem already. We knew the skull was very fragile. It was the largest element we had yet attempted to bring out of the Chamber, and we worried about how we were going to get it through the Chute safely. Someone found a plastic lunch box: Would it fit through the Chute? Yes.

But the skull was curved, and even packed in bubble wrap and foam, it might simply collapse under its own weight. Our solution? A blue plastic cereal bowl, nested inside the lunch box.

Around 2:30 that afternoon, John called down to the team members in the cave. "Look, guys, let's think about wrapping it up for the day in around a half hour or so," he said. "I don't think you're going to be in a position to get that skull. Let's get it tomorrow."

"You know, we're feeling pretty good down here. Give us another hour or so," came the reply.

An hour later, John called down to the cave came again. "It's been an hour, and I need you to be ready to come up—you've got quite a climb ahead of you. You can have the first shift tomorrow, if you want, and get the skull then."

"We're not coming out of here without this skull," said Becca.

"Hey, I hear you," said John. "But it's time to knock it off for the day."

The intercom was silent, then Becca's voice again: "Are you going to come down here and get us?"

That settled it. It really was Skull Day.

In the end, it took more than another hour.

We watched the video feed nervously as Becca and Marina maneuvered the all-important cereal bowl into place. Patience and persistence paid off: The skull was ready to come out of the cave. They lifted and supported the partial skull as if they were moving a sick patient onto the operating table.

Everyone had been waiting for this moment. All cavers and excavators on hand took up stations along the way: at the top of the Dragon's Back, at the bottom of the ridge, at either end of Superman's Crawl, down the Ladder, and out the entrance. The skull came up the Chute in its lunch box, and from there, the team operated like a bucket brigade, passing the precious fossil hand to hand through the climbs and squeezes. Aboveground, we watched the progress on the video feeds, seeing the incredible teamwork as the skull moved out the route our teams had taken into the Chamber. Near the entrance, everyone paused to wait for Becca and Marina to catch up, and they emerged together with the skull, triumphant.

It was a great moment, capping off an entire week of great moments. Our team had gradually become aware that something extraordinary was happening. By the end of that remarkable first week, we had recovered more than 200 individual hominin fossils. That was more hominin bones than we had yet recovered from Malapa over the five years of work there. And we were literally just scratching the surface. At that point, we had not yet dug more than three inches deep, and only in an area of the cave floor hardly larger than a couple of dinner plates.

By the end of the second week, the collection had grown to more than 700 remains. That was a special number, because it exceeded the volume of the richest hominin site in Africa, Sterkfontein—a site so close I could see the entrance to its visitors center, just up the valley, from where I sat in the Command Center. Here we were, surrounded by the famous fossil sites of South Africa, where people had explored for fossils more than 70 years, and we had uncovered a site richer than any of the others. It was beyond remarkable.

I had planned the entire expedition to last three weeks. After the recovery of the first skull that Friday, two weeks remained. Some of the scientists and volunteers had to go home, including Steve Churchill, who left reluctantly for an obligation in the States. Others joined us, including Darryl de Ruiter from Texas A&M University, who had been a key member of the *sediba* team describing the skull, and Scott Williams from New York University, a specialist on vertebrae who had described the *sediba* spine remains. New members of the caving society joined us, too, and many close friendships formed between scientists and cavers during the three-week expedition.

All in all, it was the best expedition of my life. All continued to run smoothly, with only a couple small incidents, none catastrophic. Alia was injured one day as she came up the Chute, but not too seriously, thank goodness. She needed a few stitches, and I think today she is rather proud of the small scar. Our efforts on social media from the site meant that thousands of people around the world were tracking our team's progress underground. More and more, teachers were giving their classrooms daily updates, fellow anthropologists were sharing what we were doing, and curious members of the public were reading our expedition blog. People around the world were hearing the voices of our team members, and we all enjoyed sharing our news.

ॐ

FROM THE FIRST DAYS of excavation, we all had a strong feeling that we were looking at an unusual creature. Those thighbones were like Lucy's and *sediba*'s, with long, flat necks and small heads. The molars also looked primitive, getting larger toward the back of the jaw, but all in all the teeth were small, even smaller than *sediba*'s. And we had never seen anything like that metacarpal for the thumb.

Over the next two weeks, that feeling grew. The first skull was not as complete as we had hoped. As Peter carefully took it from its lunch box and reconstructed it, we could see that the brain was very small, maybe the size of an orange. And we were sad to see none of the face was there. We didn't need to wait long for more evidence from the skull, though. As the painstaking excavation exposed more of the Puzzle Box area, the team uncovered two more partial jawbones. One of them—the jawbone of a very old individual with teeth worn completely down to their roots—was nested within another partial skull, this one preserving the top of the left eye socket, including a thin browridge sticking out from the forehead. Peter put the pieces of this skull back together, and now we could see the form of the face from the eye around to behind the ear.

I sat in the Science Tent, studying the skull carefully. In profile, the skull looked like a miniature *Homo erectus*. Its browridge was thin, but separated from the forehead by a groove, and the skull was pinched inward only slightly behind the orbits. I could trace the lines of the jaw muscles on the side of the skull, back from the browridge to an angled, thick area behind the ear. No australopith had features resembling these. Yet the brain that would have been protected within this skull was clearly tiny, even smaller than that of the first skull we had unearthed. No *erectus* skull had ever been found with a brain so small. Adding further to the mystery, the back of the skull was not long and angled like an *erectus* skull at all. Instead it curved sharply, almost like the skull of a modern human.

I shook my head in wonder as I held this tiny specimen. I had never seen anything like it.

# 25

On the second-to-last day on-site, I pulled Rick and Steven aside. I hadn't forgotten my promise to them about their second possible find, the thighbone they had seen in another part of the cave. Now that the expedition had successfully worked through the field season, it was time to investigate.

"OK," I said, "take Marina and Becca and go get that bone. But I want a complete map and lots of photos before you collect it."

They were off like a flash.

Two hours later, I sat on a rock at the edge of the entrance to the cave. In my hands was the proximal end of a hominin femur, very much the same in appearance as the top end of the thighbone we had recovered from the Chamber where we had worked the past three weeks. But this bone came from another location entirely—a new chamber in an entirely different direction through the underground labyrinth, as they described it. At a place near the entrance, where a hard left would go toward the Dragon's Back chamber some 60 meters away, they had instead taken a right down a sloping passage. This new chamber seemed to have no relation to the chamber where we had originally found fossils. They were more than 100 meters apart underground, separated by long, twisting passages. The first chamber was site 101 within the Wits fossil-numbering system, and for three weeks as we cataloged fossils we had given each a number starting with 101. This new chamber would be site 102.

I couldn't believe it. Another collection of fossil hominins in the same cave system? I looked up, taking in the wide grins on their four faces. I asked the inevitable question, "Was there anything else with this?"

"A skull," was Marina's answer. Our work had just begun.

TWENTY-ONE DAYS AFTER SETTING foot at Rising Star, this team of scientists, students, and volunteers had accomplished something remarkable. Together we had recovered more than 1,300 individually numbered fossil hominin remains, an unprecedented haul by any standard, far exceeding the number discovered at any single site in Africa.

We had accomplished all this in an effort put together in only four weeks, with a team of top scientists, avid cavers, and eager students. Working in one of the most inhospitable environments any paleoanthropological expedition had ever attempted, we ended the expedition without a single serious injury.

We had planned the expedition to recover a single hominin skeleton and document its context. What we found was more than anyone had dreamed possible. We had found at least one example of nearly every bone in the body. For most bones, we had multiple copies from different individuals. Among the most numerous parts were teeth, and our assessment of the teeth and jaws that had come out of the site made clear that we had at least a dozen individuals with some very young infants, at least one very old adult, and every age category in between. Yet with all these hominin bones, the only other animal remains we found were six bones from a bird and a handful of rodent teeth. No one had ever discovered a site like this.

And there were more. Everywhere in the Chamber, our team could see bones—there must be thousands still in the sediments. As much as we wanted to continue, though, we couldn't excavate any longer. Funding was exhausted, but even more important, we needed to start the scientific study of the remains to see what we were dealing with. We needed to learn more about the fossils we had so that we could make smart decisions about how to learn more from those that still remained in the site. I had never been more proud of a team of individuals, but it was time to go home.

Furthermore, the word had gone out around the world on social media, and people were asking us the same questions we were asking ourselves. What species were we looking at? How did all those bones get into this dangerous, remote chamber? And how old were they? It would be our job over the coming months to answer these questions.

How does one set about studying such an enormous haul of fossil hominins? I sat in my office back at Wits, the fossils safely stored in a number of safes, and talked about this and other problems with John Hawks after the expedition. "I want to do something radical," I said to him.

"What do you have in mind?" he asked.

"You remember what we talked about before the expedition?"

John nodded. "You mean getting young people here to study the fossils? The more I think about the idea, the more I like it. But when we were talking about that, we were only going to have one skeleton to deal with. Now we're talking about an order of magnitude more fossils than you had with *sediba*. Nobody's ever examined this many hominin fossils all at once."

I smiled and nodded. "That makes it even more important. If we get the right young people, with the right data sets, we can do right by these new fossils and transform the field."

"That's for sure," said John. "There are so many talented people out there who are never going to get a chance to work on new fossils like these. Many of them will go on to different kinds of work, the opportunities are so scarce."

"I think it is the ultimate win-win," I said. "People who have just finished their Ph.D. research have been using the newest techniques in their research. We can deliver research with the highest impact, and we're in a position to do it in short order. We just have to get the people together."

"Well, you know I'm in. Finding the right people and getting them together is the kind of challenge I like," John said with a smile.

That afternoon, I called up Albert van Jaarsveld. He had approved emergency funding from the South African National Research Foundation back in 2008 to kick-start the Malapa program of research. Now I was back again, hat in hand, to find a way to fund the analysis of the Rising Star fossils.

"I want to run a symposium," I explained. "I want to engage early career scientists, in combination with the existing *sediba* team, to study the Rising Star finds."

Albert thought about this for a moment as I waited patiently on the other end of the line for his response. "Can you call it a workshop?" he asked.

"Sure!" I said, smiling into the telephone. "I can call it anything you want!"

In early January, I posted another message on Facebook.

The University of the Witwatersrand, through the Centre of Excellence in Palaeosciences and the Evolutionary Studies Institute, will be holding a unique workshop to study and describe recently discovered fossil early hominin material for a series of high-impact publications. It is intended that the workshop will be held in South Africa from early May until the first week of June 2014.

We are seeking early career scientists with data and skill sets applicable to the study of any part of the anatomy of early hominins. Participants must be willing to share these data and skills in a collaborative workshop designed to study, describe, and publish these important hominin fossils.

The intent of the workshop is to give a unique opportunity to early career scientists to participate in the primary description of African early hominin material. Applicants must be able to attend the entirety of the workshop. Successful applicants will have all travel and accommodation costs covered; be given access to existing comparative fossils, modern material, and all data sets; and receive mentoring throughout the process from senior established scientists.

Output will include authorship on at least one high-impact paper as well as continued collaboration and authorship on future research to which he/she contributes. Interested applicants should submit their CVs, a brief summary of their skills or data sets that would be applicable to such a project (not to exceed 1,500 words), and three letters of support from established scientists in the field.

In short order we received applications from more than 150 scientists, each one bringing a different set of expertise to bear. Consulting with several of the *sediba* scientists and squeezing the funding as much as possible, we were able to select more than 30 young scientists to participate in the workshop. They would all come to Johannesburg in early May 2014 and spend five weeks together to work on the fossils firsthand.

IN THE MEANTIME, THERE was one more thing that I couldn't take care of alone. When we ended the expedition in November, we knew that we were only touching the very surface of what was left within the 101 Chamber. That wasn't just an expression. As we ended excavation work on the last day, the underground team had exposed the teeth of an upper jaw—a maxilla. We could see it there in the video feeds, slowly emerging from the sediment as they worked on it that last afternoon—at first just the teeth, then the lower part of the face. The thin bones of the face are so fragile that we didn't dare rush, and this maxilla lay within the Puzzle Box, so that as team members worked slowly downward, they exposed yet other bones that overlay part of it. There was no helping the situation. We weren't sure how complete this face might be, and the clock had run out. For its safety, we left it in place.

In March 2014, I invited Becca and Marina back to Rising Star to bring that maxilla out of the cave. If we wanted the best chance of understanding the anatomy of the face, we needed to retrieve it before our team began to analyze the fossils.

As they worked to remove it, they found just beneath it many more fragments of the skull and the complete jawbone. The upper and lower jaws fit together perfectly—the upper teeth had been worn down exactly where they had been in contact with the lower teeth in the living individual.

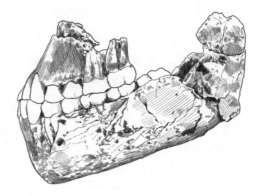

*Matching upper and lower jaw from the Rising Star cave*

Here, just inches below the surface, the bones were incredibly well preserved. In November, the team had uncovered an ankle and part of a foot in anatomical position, articulated with each other. That indicated that the leg had been deposited in the site with soft tissue holding the bones together. Up to that point, we had been working on a jumble of bones, missing many of the most fragile parts. But now, Marina and Becca were finding thin pieces of bone—the jawbone of a young child, for example. They uncovered some finger bones and slowly exposed what turned out to be a complete, articulated hand. It lay within the sediment in a death grip—fingers curled—and lacked only one tiny bone of the wrist. It was the most complete hand of a fossil hominin ever discovered. A nearly complete foot was there as well, and several partial feet, hands, and other articulated parts.

The two weeks of work in March recovered another 300 or so specimens, but they were among the most impressively complete remains that we had found so far. They would play a key role when the workshop assembled in May to study the fossils.

# PART IV
# Understanding
## *naledi*

❧

# 26

It was the first day of the workshop, and I was briefing the group. We had pulled together a great mix of early career and more senior scientists, all of whom had come together in Johannesburg to study the Rising Star assemblage of fossils. Our deputy vice chancellor of research had just welcomed the group to Wits, and now I was introducing the goals of the workshop.

"We are going to describe these fossils without a date," I told them.

A laboratory full of scientists stared back at me. A few probably thought I was joking, but most had looks of disbelief. Ever since the application of more sophisticated dating methods at Olduvai Gorge, almost every discovery of a fossil hominin in Africa had been accompanied by some kind of date. For many scientists, geological age had become a kind of insurance policy. After all, the lack of a clear idea of the geological age of the Taung Child had been part of why Raymond Dart had faced early criticism. In the popular mind, and in the minds of many paleoanthropologists, the geological age of a fossil is the key to interpreting its place in human evolution. I was telling a roomful of scientists that we were going to blindfold ourselves to that key to understanding.

In part, this decision came from necessity. Our geological team, led by Paul Dirks, had been involved with interpreting the site from the start. It was clear to everyone that it would be difficult to work out the age of the fossils in the 101 Chamber.

At Malapa, we had enjoyed a run of geological good luck. The fossils there had been sandwiched neatly between flowstone layers, and we were able to use that material to date the skeletons precisely. The nonhuman animal bones (which included saber-toothed cats, hyenas, antelopes, and a horse) gave evidence that confirmed the age of the site as determined by the flowstones.

No such luck at Rising Star. To begin with, there were only the bird bones and rodent fragments, and none of these seemed to be preserved in the same way as the hominin fossils. Unlike at Malapa, these bones were not embedded in a hard breccia with flowstone draped over the top or bottom—they were in a mass of soft, loose sediment. Bits of flowstone had eroded against the wall, but it would be hard to determine how these formations related to the fossils. Still, we tried to determine the flowstone ages using the same dating method that had worked at Malapa, but here it failed. The thin, eroded flowstones had been contaminated to some degree by sediments in the Chamber, and we had no way of knowing how long the fossils had been in the cave before the flowstone formed. Only the bottom of the Chamber floor could give us a way to use geological testing to figure out the maximum age of the fossils.

All in all, it was a problem. One day, I had spoken over Skype with Paul and his young colleague, Eric Roberts. "You are going to have to sacrifice some material to get a date," Paul told me.

"I can't do that until it's described," I replied, "and even then, you know there is no direct dating method that's likely to give us a date on this material—it's probably too old."

The logical method to try was electron spin resonance (ESR) dating, a method that uses the atomic structure of crystals formed as teeth fossilize to gauge how long a tooth has been buried. But there were two problems. First, the geologist has to know the radiation levels of the environment where the teeth were buried, and these measurements can be misleading. Worse, this analysis requires that a sample of enamel be removed from the tooth. Usually, that's not a problem, because we can sample teeth from nonhominin animals found at the site. Dating an antelope tooth is just as good as dating a hominin tooth as long as they clearly come from the same geological situation. But the 101 Chamber had no teeth from fauna—only hominins. To date them, we would have to drill into some of these precious teeth—not an option. None of us knew what these hominins were, and destroying any of these fossils before describing them would be the wrong scientific choice.

☙

THE MORE I THOUGHT about it, the more I realized that what seemed like a barrier was actually an opportunity. There was a real advantage to analyzing these fossils without dating them. We were about to study this set of extraordinary fossils. Our assessment of them would depend on their anatomy alone. They might be very similar to some other collections of fossils and very different from others. Some of those similarities would be shared with very distant common ancestors—so-called "primitive" traits—while others would be unique and distinctive features—"derived" traits. The pattern of traits would tell us their relationships—not the age of the fossils. If our collection of fossils from the 101 Chamber shared many derived traits with one particular species of hominin, we might assign them to that species. If we could not show such a pattern with any existing collection, we might name a new species. These relationships had nothing whatsoever to do with the fossils' age. So the fact that we would not know their age was not a drawback—it was an advantage!

Our team had begun to learn this lesson with *sediba*. The fossil skeletons that we had found at Malapa were possibly the best dated fossils in all of Africa. We had imagined that the highly precise dating of the site was a scientific triumph. In some ways it was, adding much more information to our knowledge of the time line of sites in the Cradle. Still, that date had also caused us some unexpected trouble.

When we described *sediba* for the first time, we emphasized that its anatomy was a mosaic—a combination of traits, some like *Homo,* others like *Australopithecus* or other primitive hominins. We thought that this species did not belong to *Homo,* but we could not deny that some comparisons placed it as a close relative. The combination of features made *sediba* look like what we might expect in an ancestor of *Homo*. It connected the primitive body plan of australopiths with more humanlike features of our genus. The mosaic of features suggested that *sediba* might be an ancestor of humans.

This seemed fairly innocuous to our team, but some other scientists asserted that it was impossible for *sediba* to be the ancestor of *Homo*. The fossils were not old enough. They pointed to a fossil found in Ethiopia that seemed to come from a rock layer 2.33 million years old. This was a mere fragment of a jaw, but its finders supported the idea that this was the earliest specimen of *Homo* ever found. The Malapa skeletons were only 1.977 million years old. It was obvious, some scientists claimed: *sediba* was simply too young to have been the ancestor of *Homo*. This was exactly the same logic by which Arthur Keith argued against the importance of the Taung Child back in 1925. If the fossil was not old enough, it could have no place in the ancestry of humans.

This logic was based on the assumption, though, that the Malapa fossils represented the earliest possible evidence of their species. Paleontology doesn't work that way. We found some individuals of *sediba* at Malapa, but other members of *sediba* almost certainly lived much earlier—how much earlier, no one could say. But in paleontology, the individuals we find as fossils are literally fewer than one in a million of the individuals that ever existed. Did *sediba* exist early enough to give rise to a 2.33-million-year-old fossil? The fossil record could not answer that question either way.

To the *sediba* team this argument about dates was beside the point. The fossil skeletons from Malapa were the best evidence from any early humanlike australopith species. If we were going to learn how our ancestors took the path toward humanity, we needed to use evidence from this branch of the family tree. Whether *sediba* itself gave rise to *Homo*, or whether instead *sediba* and early *Homo* both emerged from some other species that was their shared ancestor, the fossils provided the best clues we had to know how our evolution had happened. Dates didn't necessarily help us to understand the relationships of fossils. In the case of *sediba*, the dates were getting in the way.

So I was eager to see the team study these new fossils without any preconceptions about their age, and I convinced almost everyone of the advantages of this approach. Some workshop scientists who hadn't been involved with the *sediba* project did raise their eyebrows at first. But as they encountered the fossils, they found that not knowing their age gave them the freedom to explore ideas they might never have considered otherwise. If the anatomy of these fossils did not tell us how they were connected to our family tree, no single number representing their age would ever help. On the other hand, if their anatomy gave us a fairly clear picture of relationships, the age of the fossils, when we determined it, might serve to test some of the most cherished assumptions held by scientists in the field.

That would be worth seeing.

# 27

And so the workshop participants set to work. Each attendee contributed expertise on a different part of the body or a different type of analysis, and they formed small teams: a team for the skulls and mandibles, a team for the teeth, a team for the feet and ankles, and so on. The plan was to prepare just over a dozen papers that would describe each aspect of the body in these new fossils, all at once. The members of the *sediba* team brought hands-on experience with the fossil hominin skeletons, and the workshop scientists who were new to the team had some of the most current data sets and techniques available.

We had gone out of our way to invite some scientists representing schools of thought or research teams that had been critical of our earlier *sediba* work. We wanted them to challenge our ideas and force us to question our own assumptions. During the expedition, we had developed some hypotheses about the fossils, but now the teams would compare each body part with the entire fossil record for that part. We knew from *sediba* that we couldn't assume anything. The shape of the skull doesn't necessarily tell you what the pelvis or the foot will look like.

We went to work in the new Phillip Tobias Primate and Hominid Fossil Laboratory. Phillip had passed away in 2012, too soon to see the *sediba* discovery, but the new fossil laboratory was a great tribute to his many contributions to the science. Three of its walls were lined with deep, glass-encased shelves. The first held the university's remarkable collection of discoveries from nearly a century of South African paleoanthropology: the Taung Child, more than 500 specimens from Sterkfontein, the fossils Raymond Dart had found at Makapansgat, hominin remains from other sites, and the teeth from Gladysvale, among others.

A second wall held comparative material gathered by Phillip and others over the years: copies of fossil discoveries from other parts of the world; reconstructions of fossil specimens from Sterkfontein and Swartkrans; and ape, human, and monkey skulls of all ages, used for comparing anatomies. The vault contained almost every fossil cast we would need to study the anatomy of the new fossils: the Wits collection, filled in with loans from more than a dozen institutions that we would have on hand for the month.

A third wall had shelving meant to accommodate the next 50 years of new discoveries. The two *sediba* skeletons, in their protective cases, took up a small section of the cabinets. Days before, the fossils from Rising Star had been moved into the vault with the others. Row upon row of plastic storage trays filled the shelves, holding more than 1,500 fossil specimens, more than the rest of the fossil collection put together.

Once the lab stations were set up—"Hand Land" and "The Tooth Booth," read signs posted by two of the teams—the fossils began to come out. Teams started working through the collection, piece by piece. The silence of concentration was punctuated by moments of surprise: "Wait a minute, what is that?" "Do you think that's a piece of navicular?" Workshop scientists had their hands full, confirming identifications and describing every fragment. Even the least represented area, the pelvis, had more than 40 fragments in the collection. In the end, we had 150 hand and wrist bones, 190 teeth and pieces of tooth root, and more than 100 foot and ankle bones. The teams would closely scrutinize every last fragment for important features that could help diagnose these new fossils.

John Hawks and I acted initially as roving scientists, surveying the whole picture of research from all the different groups. The teams worked at their stations, learning all they could about the Rising Star fossils and comparing them with every piece of fossil material from South Africa, research casts of fossils from the rest of the world, and their own data sets, including measurements and digital models of still more fossils. After a week, each team briefed us on what the fossils had begun to tell them. We had developed some ideas as the bones came out of the ground. Now added data showed that many of our initial impressions were accurate—but there were other things we didn't expect.

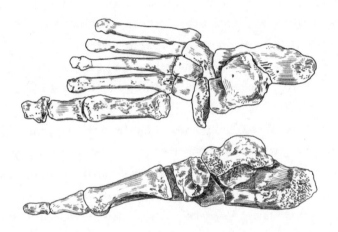

*The most complete foot from the Rising Star site.*
*Bones of the four smaller toes are not depicted here.*

The clearest example came from the foot team. Its four key scientists had more than a hundred bones to work with, and together they were able to put together parts of six feet. Considering what we knew about the skulls and teeth, we expected to hear that the foot bones would have a mix of features representative of different species, and that some interesting detail would set the Rising Star feet apart, just as the odd heel bone had for the *sediba* foot. So, it was surprising to hear that the Rising Star foot bones were nearly indistinguishable from those of modern human feet. These feet were different from the earliest bipeds, like *afarensis,* which were a bit flatter than ours, with longer toes. They didn't match *sediba.* And they were more humanlike than the single crocodile-bitten foot from Olduvai Gorge that most scientists attributed to *Homo habilis.* The feet from the 101 Chamber were essentially human. Could this species, even with its small brain, be closer to humans than *habilis* was?

The hand told a more complicated story. Again, we had more than a hundred bones, including the star of the entire collection: the nearly complete hand uncovered by Becca and Marina during their March excavation work. Tracy Kivell, who had worked to describe the hand anatomy of *sediba,* was here at the workshop examining the Rising Star hand and wrist bones. She noticed right away the unusual thumb bone that all of us had seen in the field. "That first metacarpal is really weird," she said. "I've never seen anything like it." It was becoming a common refrain.

We had recovered seven copies of that bone from the cave, and all of them were alike: a first metacarpal unlike that of any other species. Humans have long and relatively powerful thumbs, and that means our wrists have to work differently from those of the great apes. We use our thumbs to grip things against the other fingers—especially in a pinching grip against the index finger. In prehistoric humans, those powerful grips were essential to making stone tools.

The *sediba* thumb had been tremendously long—longer even than in humans today. It was in a way hyperhuman. The tips of its finger bones were broad, likely supporting big fingertip pads. All in all, the *sediba* hand looked like it had the humanlike capacity to grip things powerfully. But the MH2 hand—the hand from the second Malapa individual— lacked several of the bones of the wrist, and what was there suggested that the index finger was not as well anchored to grip against the thumb as in humans.

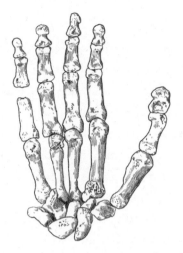

*The most complete of the hand remains from Rising Star.*
*The thumb is long, with a powerful metacarpal at its base.*

The Rising Star hand had nearly all of the wrist bones, and they told a different story. The key is a small bone called the trapezoid, wedged between the base of the thumb and index finger. A chimpanzee trapezoid is shaped a bit like a pyramid—despite the bone's name, it comes to an apex like a triangle, not a trapezoid. In humans, it lives up to its name, shaped as if someone took a cube of clay and pinched it halfway up the sides, making it into a little boot. That pinched part of the bone opens up onto the palm side of the wrist, where it helps stabilize the thumb and index finger when they grip each other. The Rising Star trapezoid bone was shaped like a human's. Also, the fingertips were very broad—broader even than those of living humans—and the thumb was not quite *sediba* length, but still quite long for a human. Thumb, wrist, and fingertips all agreed—the hand was even more human than *habilis,* and more human than the hand of the Flores hominin skeleton.

There was a catch. As the team studied the finger bones, they found that they were strikingly curved—almost as if they had gripped around a log and melted into a curved shape. That kind of curvature developed in apes as a result of long use grasping branches, in contrast to humans, who developed very flat finger bones. The Rising Star hand was humanlike in its wrist and fingertips, but the fingers seemed to be made for climbing. The shoulder was built for climbing, too. As another team worked to understand the upper body—the shoulder blade, the collarbone, the upper part of the rib cage, and the bone of the upper arm—they found that the shoulders had been canted upward, the arms oriented for climbing. The feet and parts of the hands seemed more humanlike, but the fingers and shoulders were as primitive in appearance as the earliest known hominins—apelike species like *Ardipithecus ramidus*.

The legs, hips, and trunk told their own stories. As we had observed in the field, the neck and head of the femur were very much like those of australopith species—similar to *sediba* or *afarensis*—yet there were two ridges on the femur necks that we had never seen before in any other species. The pelvis would prove to match these long femur necks with a wide, flaring hip very much like Lucy's, and the lower part of the rib cage seemed well suited for such a flaring pelvis. The spine was another story—each vertebra was relatively small, but with a relatively large canal for the spinal cord. The team had never seen this combination of vertebral traits before except in one form of hominin—the Neanderthals.

The picture emerging from the skull was equally mixed, but it took a bit longer to put together. Peter Schmid had gone back to work in his basement laboratory. In a white lab coat, he did the precise work that he loved, piecing together fragments to slowly reveal the shapes of bones and body. After a week, Peter had reconstructed almost all of the braincase of this skull—from the incredibly well-preserved rear, where the muscles of the neck had left their markings, up to the forehead. With the nearly complete mandible and left half of the upper jaw, the skull was the most beautiful example the collection had yet produced. Peter brought it into the fossil vault, beaming with satisfaction. It was a beautiful thing. The cranial team crowded around their station, looking at the four disconnected pieces of this nearly complete skull and wishing they had the parts to connect them.

ᡐᠣ

THE LABORATORY THAT MONTH was full of laser scanners. The workshop scientists had brought more than 10 of them and had set them up on every spare tabletop. Each scanner shot a red laser line out in front of a camera, recording the three-dimensional shape of a bone by slowly tracing the line across the bone surface. Many times, the lab would fall completely silent, 20 or more people working quietly at their stations, with hardly a sound except for the periodic whir of a laser turntable. After a half hour, a complete three-dimensional model would appear on the linked computer screen.

Heather Garvin, a forensic anthropologist from Mercyhurst University and part of the cranial team, had been scanning parts of the skull and jawbones. One day, she opened her laptop. "See what you think of this," she said. There it was, on the screen, not in pieces anymore but reconstructed into the shape of a complete skull. It took our breath away.

"Turn it sideways, to show the lateral view," said Peter. "There, very good, not bad, not bad. But I think the mandible and maxilla should be rotated slightly lower. Here, like this one."

Peter opened his own laptop. On the screen was the skull. He had taken photographs of each piece, at scale and in correct anatomical orientation, and had used Photoshop to elaborately move the pieces into their correct positions. And unlike the slightly cartoonlike three-dimensional model, this one showed the skull in stunning photographic detail. Again, our jaws dropped. The two reconstructions—one with old technology, and one with new—were a near match.

The virtual reconstruction allowed Heather to estimate the volume within the skull, which corresponds approximately to the size of the brain. It was around 560 cubic centimeters, about the size of many larger male australopith skulls, and at the small end for *Homo habilis*. We now thought the smaller skull we had recovered in the field, with its thin browridge, was probably a female. Its volume was smaller, around 450 cubic centimeters, the size of many female australopiths and just a bit bigger than the beautifully complete MH1 skull of *sediba,* a juvenile male.

The size itself was not a surprise. Ever since I had held that first portion of the skull—the fossil mandible Marina and Becca had first brought up—it was obvious it was going to be a small one. But its size did not seem to match its anatomy. That thin, little browridge, sticking out from the forehead like a mini-shelf, made it look like a tiny *Homo erectus* skull.

In fact, it looked quite a lot like skulls found in Dmanisi, in the Republic of Georgia. There, five skulls and assorted other parts of skeletons had been found during the past 20 years, all assigned to the species *Homo erectus.* An estimated 1.8 million years old, the Dmanisi remains were the earliest hominin remains ever discovered outside of Africa, and possibly the earliest examples of *Homo erectus* anywhere. The five Dmanisi skulls were small for *erectus,* the smallest close to that found in the 101 Chamber, with a brain size of 550 cubic centimeters, and the others from 600 up to 750 cubic centimeters. Other bones were there as well, representing an anatomy that was, in some ways, primitive for *erectus*—with their small brain, body just about the size of a human pygmy, and fairly thin cranial bones.

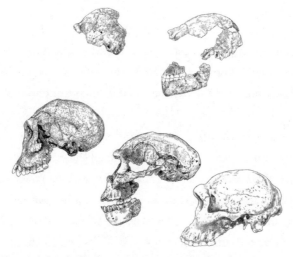

*Three of the skulls from Dmanisi at the bottom, compared*
*with two partial skulls from Rising Star at top*

Dmanisi was a very important comparison for us. As the cranial team worked, they began to compare measurements of the shape of the skull, finding that the Dmanisi skulls were among the closest examples to our Rising Star cranial sample. Yet other characteristics were closer to species that had branched earlier in our family tree, including *Homo habilis* and *Homo rudolfensis*. The tooth team was finding, for example, that the teeth of the 101 Chamber hominins seemed to fit with those of species like *erectus, habilis,* and *rudolfensis*—but they did not have all the features of any of those species, and they had several features that clearly distinguished them from each.

Other distinctive aspects of the Rising Star species were coming to light. People sometimes ask us how we know that all the bones from the 101 Chamber really represent a single kind of hominin. The answer is in the incredible similarity of the bones that we found. That strange form of the first metacarpal, for example, was shared by seven different examples of the bone found in the Chamber. The front lower premolar also had a strange form that we had never seen in other hominins, and again every example from the site showed the same set of features. The sizes of the bones and teeth were all very much alike. This implied not only that the bones might come from a single population, but also that the amount of difference between adult males and females was quite small.

The measurements coming from the different teams allowed us to estimate the size of the adult body: weight between 90 and 120 pounds, height from four feet six inches to five feet. In other words, they were the size of very small-bodied humans today. The teeth told us that we had brought at least 15 individuals out of the cave, although with all the bones remaining in the cave—maybe thousands—we suspected there are many more. These 15 individuals included at least eight children of various ages, from infants to adolescents. And one older adult, with teeth worn down to the roots, had probably reached the late 30s or older.

GRADUALLY, DIFFERENT TEAMS BEGAN to compare notes. Over the next week, I heard many gasps and some nervous giggling, and I saw a lot of head shaking. Nothing was adding up to any species we knew already. The feet seemed like human feet. The shoulders were like those of some primitive hominin. But almost every other part of the skeleton was a mosaic. The blades of the hip bones—the ilia—were like Lucy's, but the lower pelvis—the ischia—was more like a human's. The hands had humanlike wrists and curved fingers. The teeth had primitive proportions but were like modern human teeth in size. Overall, everyone quickly came to the same conclusion: We had not only a new hominin species but also one that showed a mosaic of morphologies—a combination of body characteristics that had never before been seen in any other species.

With *sediba*, we had faced a similar scenario, which came down to the difficult question of which genus we should choose for the fossils: *Homo*, like us, or *Australopithecus*, like much more primitive fossil species. Here, with the Rising Star fossils, we had the same question. But in this case, the solution seemed easier. *Sediba* had a face and hips like humans, but in most aspects of its body, it was like australopiths—and a few features were even like those of apes. The Rising Star fossils shared three key features with *Homo*: Their hands were well suited for manipulating objects, and probably tool-making—even more so than species like *Homo habilis* or *Homo floresiensis*. Their teeth were adapted for a high-quality diet, like all members of *Homo*. Their body size, and in particular their legs and feet, were humanlike. All three were key aspects of the way that humans and our close relatives have worked, moved, and lived within the environment. Besides this, the shape and features of the skull were distinctly humanlike. The small brain and primitive features of the skeleton were important, but they did not detract from the overall picture.

This was *Homo*.

# 28

"All right, then, what is its name?" Several of us were sitting around the breakfast table when Steve Churchill asked the question. It was time. With *sediba,* we had batted around ideas, listening to the sound of them and shooting them down, until we came to one that seemed to fit.

Everyone looked at me. "I was thinking of *naledi,*" I said. "It's Sesotho for 'star'—Rising Star. And we need a name for the 101 Chamber. I think we should call it the 'Dinaledi Chamber'—that's plural—it means 'stars.'"

The others agreed. "*Homo naledi,*" Steve said. "I like the sound of it."

Now we had named the creature that the bones represented—a new species, never discovered before. This declaration spun out a new string of mysteries, though, some familiar to us after the work on *sediba.* We already had proposed, just six years ago, that here in the Cradle, after more than 70 years of intensive exploration for hominin ancestors, we were adding a new species to the picture of human evolution. Now, it seemed, we had a second new species, represented by fossils in great abundance. Missing one species could be chalked up to bad luck. But missing two species started to look like a pattern. Only a tiny part of Africa had been subjected to the sort of intense paleoanthropological exploration that had brought *sediba* and *naledi* to view. What more could be out there waiting for us to find?

That question would have to wait, because now our team was fully occupied with another: How did the bodies get into the cave?

༟

TOWARD THE END OF the workshop, Eric Roberts, Paul Dirks's young colleague, arrived to help with the geological study of the site. Eric had come to collect more data from inside the cave, helping us understand how the Rising Star system was put together. Only by knowing more about the geology of the cave would we be able to establish how the fossils got into the Chamber. It had become our habit when starting to work with other scientists to size people up, literally, to see if they might be able to fit down the Chute. Eric had the right skill set and, importantly, the right physique. He would be our geologist inside the Dinaledi Chamber.

Our team had found soft chunks of reddish orange clay interspersed in some areas with the fossils, their color standing out in comparison to the dark brown sediment. Eric determined that the orange clay was in the Chamber first, before the *naledi* fossils were deposited there. Pieces of it still adhere to the walls of the Chamber, he observed, and as the fossil deposit formed, bits of the orange clay fell into the younger sediments. We had found traces of tiny rodents in the sediments around the fossils—mostly remnants of enamel from rodent incisors—but that was the only evidence of any kind of animal remains within the sediment where we found *Homo naledi*. Now Eric determined that these tiny pieces had probably come from the orange clay and had nothing to do with the hominin fossils at all.

The orange clay chunks told us something more. If the sediments had been carried in by water, they would have formed as a single muddy mass. Distinct chunks of the soft orange clay would never have lasted—they would have dissolved. The Chamber may have seen a gentle rise in the water table, but never a violent rush of water capable of carrying bones along with it.

Everyone on our excavation team had found the Dinaledi Chamber a silent place. Listening to the descriptions of people who had been inside, those of us on the surface had begun to imagine it as if it were a time capsule, virtually unchanged from the moment the unlucky hominins had ended up inside. But the geology suggests that the silence today is misleading. Dinaledi hadn't been a peaceful place at all. It had a dramatic history. First, the Chamber had been partially filled with the orange clay material. Then, that was mostly removed—possibly washed out in the distant past, or slowly percolated downward through small drains in the floor of the Chamber. Later, the hominin remains came into the cave. These were slowly covered by a fine, chocolate brown sediment that made up the majority of the fossil deposit we had dug.

But there was more. The *naledi* fossils were embedded in the brown sediment that made up the floor of the Chamber, but Eric found clear evidence that this material had once extended much farther up the walls. In some areas, dripping water had created small deposits of calcium carbonate—flowstones—on top of the brown sediment floor. Some of the flowstones were now clinging to the walls of the Chamber, many inches above the current floor level, their edges broken where they had grown too thin to support their own weight. The conclusion was clear: The surface of the floor containing the hominin fossils was once higher. Floor drains were still at work, and sediment had been seeping down out of the Chamber, possibly carrying bits of *Homo naledi* with it.

During our excavation work so far, we had not given much attention to the Landing Zone, the area of the Chamber directly below the Chute. The team had found a few fossils in the area, including one tooth, but we had not excavated there. Eric found the area to be of key importance. A series of flowstones clung to the wall, tracing a record of ancient surfaces where water had dripped. Beneath and between them were remnants of sediment with bits of fossil bone. This area, the highest in the Chamber, seemed to represent a layer of the site that was now mostly gone, a layer that had once been above the present floor of the Chamber. This discovery made it very unlikely that the hominins could have arrived all at once in a single event.

We had seen other clues suggesting that the bones had entered the Chamber over some period of time and not as the result of a single mass death.

For instance, as the team slowly worked down through the Puzzle Box, they had followed the path of a single femur downward through the sediment. For more than a week, they continued to excavate, never reaching the bottom of this bone, because it was vertically implanted, surrounded by hundreds of other bone fragments with a more horizontal orientation. Just as our team had to take the puzzle apart in a certain order, it seemed likely that the bones had come into the Chamber in a sequence, over time, and not all at once.

Jan Kramers had been working in his lab at the University of Johannesburg, analyzing the chemistry of the sediments around the fossils, while Eric Roberts and Paul Dirks were studying the particles and mineral fragments in the sediments. To most of us who had gone inside Rising Star, the floor of the cave, with its nondescript brown color, was just made of dirt. From one chamber to another, it might vary a bit in color and texture—in some places more rocky, in others more fine—but it was still just dirt. But the casual eye misses a complex landscape of different minerals, arrayed in pieces of different sizes. Under a microscope, these tiny mineral fragments began to show how the Dinaledi deposit had formed.

Jan found that the Dinaledi sediment samples were made up of tiny fragments of minerals rich in potassium and aluminum oxide, produced by slow weathering of the dolomite as the cave continued to form. These particles had an angular shape, with sharp edges that showed they could not have moved very far.

But when the team looked at the sediment from the floor of the Dragon's Back chamber, they found a very different picture. That sediment was rich in silicon, and it was packed with many noticeable grains of quartz—particles that must have come from the outside environment above the cave. Even though they were microscopic, the bigger pieces had rounded edges, as if they had rubbed against each other as they were carried some distance. Some of those quartz particles probably came out of the breccia that was exposed in the Dragon's Back chamber, a part of the cave whose geology both Eric and Paul had been able to examine closely.

Paul found that this part of the cave, including the tight squeeze known as Superman's Crawl, had changed over time. At some point in the past, large piles of material had spilled into this area from outside the cave, transforming a larger cavern into the tight passages we now encounter. Superman's Crawl, in other words, may not have been there when *Homo naledi* encountered the cave. One of the fills sloped all the way into the Dragon's Back, and it contained fossils of other animals. This area looked a lot more like other caves in the Cradle, and although we could not yet be sure, it seemed possible that this part of the cave might have been easier for *naledi* to get through than it is for us today.

As we quickly learned, though, "easier" does not necessarily mean "very easy." The sediment samples from the Dinaledi Chamber and Dragon's Back were very different from each other. Particles were reaching the Dragon's Back from outside the cave, tumbling some distance down through the caverns, but that sort of particle did not reach the Dinaledi Chamber. The Chamber was isolated, and always had been, so the soil around the hominin bones was distinctly different from any outside the Chamber. The ceiling of the Chamber was a solid layer of chert, with no substantial gaps or cracks that would allow a body to enter. Superman's Crawl may have been differently configured, but the Dragon's Back itself must have been in place before the bodies arrived, sealing in the Dinaledi Chamber from the outside environment, so that it was accessible only through small and indirect passages. The Chute that our team had been using was the only one of those passages large enough for anyone to get into the Chamber, now and in the age when the fossil remains were deposited.

People have often asked us whether some other entrance to the Dinaledi Chamber might have existed in the past. Another opening into the Chamber would have given *naledi* an easier route than the one our team was using, they suggest. We cannot rule out that some other entrance existed, and our geological team is still working to understand the entire cave system. But there is one thing we can say for sure: If there was any other entrance to the Chamber when *naledi* lived, it must have been just as hard to access as the

Chute is for us now. If it had ever been easy to enter, there would be signs of other animals and larger sediment particles in the Chamber. The difficult entry helps to explain the evidence we have found.

❧

As the team of anatomical specialists prepared to leave the workshop, heading off to finish their research papers, an even more detailed process of study began to unfold, bone by bone. Lucinda Backwell is what you might call a specialist in paleoforensics. The name for her work is taphonomy—the study of how fossil bone is changed by natural and artificial processes after an animal's death. She and her colleagues study fossils intensely, often poring over their surfaces using high-powered microscopes, and then they go a step further and analyze what natural agents created any tiny markings or patterns of coloration they have found. In other words, she uses science to explain what is barely visible to the eye. Lucinda had found amazing things in the fossil deposit at Malapa, including parts of plants and insects, and those findings had prompted her to study the role of termites in the formation and taphonomy of fossil sites in southern Africa.

Some of the fossil sites in the Cradle represent thousands of years of left-overs from the meals eaten by large cats, especially leopards. These cats move their prey to trees to avoid the attention of lions and hyenas—and in the Cradle landscape, trees are often found near the openings of caves. Cats leave signs of chewing on bones—tooth marks and puncture marks. Likewise, hyenas create impressive fractures and even swallow and digest pieces of bone, leaving behind fossil bones etched with stomach acid. It's an impressive sight to see a hominin fossil that has been ravaged by meat-eaters. In the Ditsong Museum in Pretoria, a fragment of skull from Swartkrans bears two puncture marks, an inch apart. The bone is displayed alongside the jaw of a leopard to show how the canine teeth match the holes perfectly.

Lucinda examined the Dinaledi bones under her microscope. Not a single one of them had any trace of a tooth mark, a puncture mark, or any other mark produced by carnivores or large scavengers. The bones preserved tiny marks from snails, which had scavenged their surfaces over the millennia to gather up calcium for their shells, but nothing from any large mammal.

At the same time, Patrick Randolph-Quinney, a forensic anthropologist, examined the breakage patterns of the bones. Fresh bones break like green tree branches, splintering along the grain of the bone tissue. When carnivores eat a carcass, that's exactly how the bones break. The strength of bone comes from its mineral content—calcium and phosphorus mostly—held together with a framework made from a protein called collagen, which strengthens the bone much like steel rebar strengthens concrete. After an animal dies, its bones slowly lose the strength provided by that protein. Eventually the bones break differently, often across the grain and in short blocks, like toppled pillars from an ancient Greek temple.

The Dinaledi bones were broken—very few of them were anywhere near complete. But across the entire collection, not a single break showed the evidence of a fresh, green fracture. In other words, these bones broke long after the individuals died. As they lay there, their collagen slowly deteriorated. Sediment piled above them and trickled through, and the bones became brittle and fractured. There was no sign of a break from a carnivore, no sign of a sudden cave-in trapping them, no sign of an individual falling into a death trap. The geology of the cave itself broke these bones long after the individuals had died.

We thought long and hard about the possibility that water had moved or accumulated the bones. The Dinaledi Chamber is not far above the water table today, and the sediments contain so much moisture that we must allow the bones to dry out slowly after we excavate them. The Malapa situation was on our minds—we knew that hominins might have entered a cave seeking water. But if the Chamber had been a pool of water in the past, those discrete chunks of red-orange clay would never have remained in the sediment. The sediment from the Dinaledi Chamber was not like the sediment around the Dragon's Back, which showed us that water did not flow downhill into the Dinaledi Chamber. We found so many body parts in perfect anatomical positions—including the complete hand and foot, several other partial hands and feet, and part of the leg of a child. That told us that these body parts must still have been enclosed in soft tissue, held together by tendons and ligaments, when they reached their current positions. If water had carried them through the cave, it would also have carried larger particles of sediment from the same area. We found the skeletons of young children, nearly every body part. These fragile bones would never have survived if a surge of water had carried them here.

At Malapa, we had proposed that the cave was a death trap—animals seeking water during a dry season might have come a bit far over the edge and fallen. The broken bones of the *sediba* individual provided solid evidence for it. Those hominins might have become trapped, one at a time, as they fell deeply from the surface. But Dinaledi was different. The sediments ruled out that the Chamber had ever been open to the outside. For *naledi* to fall into that Chamber by accident, they would first have had to delve deeply into the dark zone of the cave. We may not know for sure that they entered the Chamber through the Chute, but even if there was another entrance, it kept other animals out. In our view, the easiest way to explain the lack of other animals was that the Chamber was far enough into the dark, labyrinthine zone of the cave to exclude them.

Had *naledi* intentionally come into the depths of this cave? Back in November 2013 the idea had seemed inconceivable. Now as we pondered the strange lack of fauna and the richness of hominins at the site, it was almost inescapable. Like Sherlock Holmes, we had eliminated all the likely possibilities of how these hominin remains got into the Chamber. None of the explanations that worked for other caves in the Cradle worked for Dinaledi. The best hypothesis we had left was that *naledi* had put those bodies deliberately into the Chamber.

Some anthropologists place a special value on such behavior. It's part of how they define modern humans. For nearly a century, archaeologists had argued about whether Neanderthals recognized mortality, understood death, or buried the remains of their dead. Neanderthals were fundamentally human, with a brain size and evidence for complex culture that rivaled those of modern humans. With *Homo naledi,* though, we were looking at a primitive creature with a brain only a third the size of a human brain today. Could it be possible that this species—clearly not human— still had the kind of awareness and social complexity that we see in our own species?

As we pondered this issue, we realized how misleading it could be to assume that the behavior we were seeing was exactly like human behavior. Chimpanzees and gorillas show clear signs of distress when individuals in their groups die or go missing. The same is true of most social mammals, including elephants and dolphins. But they do not seem to share any cultural practice of tending to the bodies of the dead and leaving them in a particular place. Our relatives among the apes seem to have all the emotional abilities necessary as a foundation for such behavior. If *naledi,* indeed, had such a practice, it may have been just the first step along a cultural transformation.

We struggled to think of ways to test the idea that *naledi* deliberately deposited their dead here. No other hypotheses made as much sense. If *Homo naledi* had gathered dead bodies in a single place, their motivation did not need to be the same as recent human cultures. In fact, cultures can be starkly different from each other: Some cultures leave grave goods with bodies— special objects to accompany the dead—but others don't. Some expose the bodies for predators and scavengers to consume; others protect the bodies from those creatures. The sheer variety of possibilities made it hard to imagine a test.

Still, if *naledi* was repeatedly using the Rising Star cave system to deposit bodies, they may have spent time in other parts of the system for other purposes. We might find some evidence of habitation or other activity if we investigated other parts of the cave. If they were using the dark zone, they might have had light. That meant we might find evidence of fire.

And if this was really a behavior repeated within a *Homo naledi* population, it seemed unlikely that the Dinaledi Chamber would be the unique and only place where they had deposited bodies. If we looked, we might find other similar situations. We didn't know yet what site 102 contained. That would be our next excavation priority.

# 29

As the workshop ended, our teams were busy preparing manuscripts describing the fossils, the new species, and its geological context. This work would take many months of writing, revision, and review by other experts outside our team before the first parts were ready to publish. Initially, we decided to send an entire package of papers to the journal *Nature,* a traditional home for such studies. *Nature* had published the first description of the Taung Child, the first description of *Homo habilis,* and many other historic studies. It seemed a natural place.

But this was not meant to be. We sent a series of papers describing the Dinaledi fossils, all in support of the work defining *Homo naledi* and describing the geological context of the cave. We wanted to show that the proposed new species was supported by detailed work on anatomy across the entire skeleton. This would be a reversal of the usual approach, in which scientists describe a new species in a very short paper and only much later provide greater detail.

Apparently we took this new approach a step too far. The referees of the papers agreed that the fossils were important, but there were too many papers. Through several months of back-and-forth communications with the editor, we found that we could not find a way to publish our team's work in *Nature*. The editors fundamentally disagreed with us about the scope and scale of the reporting needed to describe this immense new collection scientifically.

Through my entire career, I have advocated for broader access to fossils. It was my early instinctive response to what I found to be a clique—a small international coterie of fossil discoverers who involved only a handful of experts in their work and talked mainly to each other. Scientists outside this group often struggled for the most basic access to data, which prevented them from doing their best possible work—a situation I deplored.

But many established paleoanthropologists acted as if open access would endanger the resources they needed to carry out their work. When I had first opened up access to the Sterkfontein fossils—now more than 15 years ago—other paleoanthropologists had strongly objected. With the *sediba* discovery, and now with *naledi,* our team was acting on the principle that open access empowered us, bringing hundreds of researchers and their resources from around the world to South Africa. Ensuring open access to the fossils has empowered the South African government to invest in the science of paleoanthropology, recognizing it as an area of scientific strength unique to the nation. The work has enabled development of the local community around the sites for tourism and support of the science, and it has given scientists the tools to make good decisions about the way forward.

Reflecting on this, we decided to do something unprecedented. We submitted our first papers describing the Rising Star fossils to *eLife,* a relatively new scientific journal that followed an open-access policy, matching the ethic that we had developed for the fossil remains themselves. Our papers would total more than 70 pages, providing six times as much supporting information as most previous papers that had described new hominin fossil discoveries. After a rigorous and collaborative review process, the papers would be published on September 10, 2015—not quite two years after

Steven and Rick first went down the Chute and found fossil bones scattered on the cave floor.

We could watch the impact of our decision to publish our findings online. In days, more than 100,000 people around the world had viewed or downloaded the scientific papers describing the discovery; over the next few months, that number grew to more than 250,000. Over the next year, the number of views and downloads topped 325,000, according to *eLife*'s own metrics.

In another unusual move, we released our scans of the fossils simultaneously. We were able to take open access to the fossils another step beyond what we had done for *sediba*, thanks to a new initiative from Duke University called MorphoSource, a website that archives data from skeletons and fossil specimens in a format that can drive three-dimensional printers. As soon as our team uploaded the data from laser scans of key Rising Star fossils to the site, our scientific colleagues and teachers around the world started downloading them. It had never happened before—almost immediately, as soon as the fossils were announced, people around the world were using 3-D printers to create and examine their own copies of them.

This kind of open access to scientific data has become common in other fields of science. Geneticists share DNA sequences even before they publish papers based on the data, and astronomers share data from telescopes and other instruments. But in the study of human evolution, this approach had never been attempted on such a scale.

With the announcement of *naledi*, not only the new species but also the open access to the science won high praise and much attention, all the way up to the highest levels. At the press conference announcing the papers, our team was joined by the deputy president of South Africa, Cyril Ramaphosa, who praised the extraordinary teamwork and skills that enabled us to carry out the challenging work and our team's commitment to open access. As he put it, these discoveries about our ancient fossil relatives help establish the scientific basis of our common humanity.

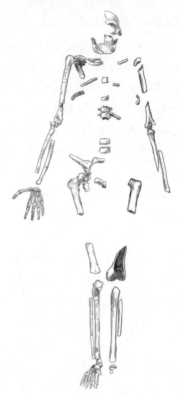

*Reconstruction of the skeleton of* Homo naledi. *The different fossils here probably come from several different individuals.*

OVER THE NEXT FEW weeks and months, I proudly watched as casts of *Homo naledi* went up on display in museums across the world. At Maropeng, the visitors center for the Cradle of Humankind World Heritage site, the university worked with the government to enable the original *naledi* fossils—hundreds of them—to go on public display. People in South Africa—families, school classes, and tourists from around the world—flocked to see this new human relative. When it was time for the fossils to return to the secure vault at the university, the museum organized a farewell concert. Around the world, more and more people were learning the story of our underground explorers and pondering the mystery of the Dinaledi Chamber. Humanity had met a new species of human relatives, and all embraced it.

Our team had seen many transitions. Six of our workshop scientists had new babies. One of the underground astronauts, Lindsay Eaves, had fallen in love and married one of the cavers, Rick Hunter, and soon they were expecting a child of their own. Others finished their Ph.D. degrees and moved on into postdoctoral or tenure-track positions. Marina Elliott, Ph.D. completed, relocated to South Africa to head the exploration team, continuing her work underground in the Rising Star cave system. The National Research Foundation recognized the entire team with their second ever award for "Team Science." All in all, Rising Star had been good to everyone.

ᏉᏉ

How did *NALEDI* change the story of human evolution?

As with *sediba,* our first publication on *naledi* was not an end but a beginning of many new lines of research. There was so much left to do.

One thing dominated our thinking as we digested the research we had accomplished already: These two samples from Malapa and Dinaledi combined gave us better evidence across the entire skeleton than any other fossil samples that we could compare them with. Only when we got to archaic humans, like Neanderthals, did we have a full enough fossil record to see the anatomy of our relatives so well.

In a lot of ways, *naledi* seemed like a logical step in a humanlike direction from *sediba.* Both of these species had small brains, australopith-like in size, but the *naledi* skull was shaped more like the skull of *Homo erectus,* with teeth that seemed more like those of *erectus, habilis,* and even archaic humans. That much was clear. *Sediba* had a primitive foot and leg; *naledi* was humanlike. *Sediba* was more humanlike in its wrist anatomy than *habilis,* but *naledi*'s hand was almost entirely like a human's, except for those curved fingers. There were some exceptions. In *sediba,* the hips were more like humans'; in *naledi,* they were more primitive, like those of the early hominins that stood and walked upright.

Five years after we had described the Malapa finds, more and more scientific work had confirmed our original idea that *Australopithecus sediba* was a close relative of *Homo*. Now, the Dinaledi fossils showed us a new hominin species—another form of *Homo* that seemed very close to what that ancestral form might have been.

But was it? Our scientific colleagues around the world wanted to know one thing more than anything else. How old were the fossils?

We were about to find out.

# 30

By February 2014 it was time to explore the chamber we had named 102, the adjacent one that Rick and Steven had told me about. They were so excited about its potential that I wanted to see for myself. The first squeeze was a tight one for me. Its two vertical walls pressed hard against my chest as I shimmied along the downward slope. Alia and Rick had gone through ahead of me, their smaller frames unbothered. John was behind me. Seeing me squeeze between the rock faces, he shrugged. "I've got some inches on you, Lee," he said. "I guess I'll sit this one out . . . again."

Now, after a few hours underground, I was coming back up the same passage, but it seemed even narrower than before. The walls wedged my body in more tightly than they had before. I couldn't get a foothold. I couldn't figure out how to move. I kept my focus, though—it reminded me of my scuba training, when you learned to respond to danger with calm analysis—and I systematically tried new ways to twist upward. It took 45 minutes of groaning and sweating until I finally popped through to freedom.

"I think from now on we'll call that one the 'Berger Box,'" said Rick. All of us stood exhausted in the shady entryway of the Rising Star cave, laughing. My face, caving gear, and clothing were all covered in grime.

That was the last time I went down to site 102, but that one trip had been well worth the struggle. The passage leading down to this new underground expedition site went almost at right angles from the passage that led to the Dinaledi Chamber. On a map, the two chambers were nearly a hundred meters apart. But they were in totally different sections of the cave system. Going from one chamber to the other underground would be much farther. There was no way that any natural processes could have moved fossils from one site to the other, and the layout of the cave made it impossible for gravity alone to have filled both sites with fossils from a single cave entryway.

And 102 was full of fossils! That day we plotted and recovered pieces of hominin skull, jawbone, and a few other fragile bits, all found exposed on the sediment surface. Our work began again, doing the same meticulous scanning, documenting, collecting, and cataloging of fossil finds from this new cave site. Marina Elliott became the primary underground astronaut in this new phase of excavation, and over the next two years she would dig one or two days at a time in this chamber, working with the exploration team and joined at one time or another by Becca, Hannah, or Elen. By 2016, they had uncovered large parts of an adult hominin skeleton, together with at least one bone from another adult as well as teeth and bones from what looked like three young children.

So what were we finding in Chamber 102? At first we did not assume that the fossils necessarily were *Homo naledi,* like those found in Dinaledi. Swartkrans cave, just a few hundred meters away, contained fossils of both *Australopithecus robustus* and some form of *Homo,* probably *erectus.* Maybe the Rising Star cave complex would also prove to be home to more than one species.

Over months, as we examined the fossils and compared them to other hominins, it became clear that 102 held remains very similar to those from the Dinaledi Chamber. The femur had the same long neck with the oval cross section. The vertebrae had the same small size, with large canals for the spinal cord. The clavicle was short and curved, just like those we had found for *naledi.* Over time the team found all 32 teeth belonging to the adult skull, and they looked just like the Dinaledi teeth, primitive in proportion, with the interesting shape of the premolars and canines. Every piece of evidence brought up from Chamber 102 suggested that these bones were *Homo naledi,* almost identical in measurements to those from the Dinaledi

Chamber. This did not seem like a coincidence. These bones looked like they all came from the same biological population.

༄

We had already faced the question of how the fossils had gotten down into the Dinaledi Chamber. Their extraordinary context—the twisting pathway underground that led to the Chamber—ruled out any easy explanations. There were no teeth marks on the fossils, so we know they had not been chewed or left there by carnivores. The mineral composition of the sediment told as they could not have been washed into the Chamber. The fossils represented at the very least dozens of individuals, ranging in age from youth to elderly, so we had to rule out the possibility that the Dinaledi Chamber contained the remains of a few unlucky *naledi* cave explorers. When we had announced the fossils to the world, a few people suggested that a *naledi* group had become lost and trapped there. Knowing the Chamber well, though, we knew that it was highly unlikely that a group including infants and young children would have ever gone there.

So what was left? Intentional deposition: a deliberate decision by this group of hominins to place their dead in this underground chamber. By a process of elimination, that was looking to be the likely answer to the question of how the bones got there. But that hypothesis, we all admitted, was extremely hard to test.

In Chamber 102, though, the context was somewhat different. Soft, fine sediment filled a small alcove, spilling out and slumping downslope. Marina and the team found hominin bones here and in another area of the chamber, but because of the erosion it was difficult to say exactly how or when they may have arrived there. No stone tools or other artifacts accompanied them. The team recovered a few bones of other animal species from the chamber, but not clearly within the sediment where they found the hominin fossils. These animals may have reached the chamber long after the hominins. We could tell that cavers had come through, and maybe other creatures had as

| 215 |

well. The passage to 102 was tight, but it was nothing like the extremely challenging Chute above the Dinaledi Chamber.

There were a lot of unanswered questions, but one thing was certain. No accident, no cave collapse, and no death trap like the one we envisioned at Malapa could account for these two chambers, far from one another within one cave system, both full of remains of the same ancient hominins. Granted, it is hard to be definitive as you make the leap between the scientific evidence and your best guess about ancient behavior. But we had formulated a hypothesis about the Dinaledi Chamber, and the 102 Chamber added important corroborating evidence. The best hypothesis to account for these fossils is that *Homo naledi* used these chambers intentionally as places to deposit their dead.

Our team is still working to uncover how *naledi* may have used the cave as a whole, and this work will undoubtedly go on for years. Even though the configuration of the two chambers suggests that they were always relatively inaccessible, there may be other areas of the cave that were once open and are now filled with sediments or breccias—areas that *naledi* might have been able to enter. We do not know yet whether they needed artificial light, as we do today, to use these caves. Maybe we will find evidence that *naledi* lived somewhere within the cave system, or used it regularly for shelter. Our exploration continues: We have found some other promising sites within the Rising Star cave system, and we will continue to investigate them to find more evidence of *naledi* or other hominins.

Our excavations in 102 helped us know *Homo naledi* even better. We recovered nearly every part of an adult skull, even the nose and the tiny parts of the eye socket that contain the tear ducts. With his typical patience and anatomical expertise, Peter Schmid reconstructed the skull, working with exquisite care upon these thin pieces. As it took shape, we began at last to see the face of *naledi.* This skull was slightly bigger, with more noticeable muscle markings, than the other *naledi* skulls we had excavated. It had well-worn teeth, suggesting that this adult male had had a long life. His face was not so broad as the face of *Homo erectus;* the bridge of his nose was flat, turning out just slightly at the bottom. His jaw must have been powerful for its small size. His face made him seem almost human, but he had that same tiny brain and primitive teeth we knew so well from the individuals found in the Dinaledi Chamber.

൦൦

WE STILL HAD TO answer the question of how old the *Homo naledi* fossils were. For that, we needed to turn to the geologists. Over the same months that we were exploring Chamber 102, our team of geologists was busy analyzing the flowstone—the thin mineral coating found throughout the Dinaledi Chamber. Earlier they had attempted to date the flowstone samples by the technique that had been so successful at Malapa, but the mineral content of the Dinaledi flowstone demanded a different process. Analysis of the thin flowstone residues on the Chamber walls above the fossil-bearing sediment indicated that they were less than 250,000 years old. But that just told us that the fossils had to be older than that—no surprise. We needed a way to find an upper limit—a maximum age—without destroying any more of the precious fossil material than we had to.

For that the team turned to electron spin resonance (ESR), the technique that helps date fossils by analyzing how long-term exposure to radiation changes the electron energy within crystals, including those in tooth enamel. By this time we were willing to sacrifice a few *naledi* fossils for the sake of dating our finds. We sent three teeth that had been brought up from the Dinaledi Chamber to be zapped with lasers, drilled, and sampled. The ESR assessment of all three teeth indicated that these hominin remains are less than 450,000 years old.

So now we had our age range for *Homo naledi:* These fossils must come from a time between 450,000 and 250,000 years ago. The time range may seem broad, but to a paleoanthropologist, it makes very little difference whether *naledi* was in the Rising Star cave system 450,000 or 250,000 years ago. This hominin's anatomy had our colleagues—and ourselves!—guessing that the fossils might be nearly two million years old. Now we had discovered that they are vastly younger than anyone assumed.

Now we understood why the *naledi* fossils were so well preserved, and why in both chambers we had found them in soft, unconsolidated sediments instead of hard breccia. We were lucky to have found them before erosion destroyed the deposits altogether. Explorers didn't look for fossils in places like these. I had worked in caves for years, and whenever I saw bone fragments in soft sediments on the cave floors, I tended to dismiss them. Those dusty bones had to be too recent—surely not interesting, I used to think. Who knows how many other troves of important fossils might have once existed in caves like this—or might still exist, waiting to be discovered?

༉༚

FROM *SEDIBA* TO *NALEDI:* All along the way, behind all the research and analysis of the findings from Malapa and Rising Star, lay the question of the origin of *Homo,* the line of hominin species that ultimately led to *Homo sapiens,* humans of today. How did these two new species relate to us? Were these our direct ancestors or offshoots of the human family tree that died out while our ancestors thrived? The ESR dating of *naledi* made the answers to these questions more challenging—and more interesting.

The hominin fossil record tells us that the species that most closely resemble *naledi,* like *Homo habilis* or early members of *Homo erectus,* lived more than 1.5 million years ago. Long after that, more humanlike species appeared—species that we assumed were the immediate ancestors of modern humans. Now the Rising Star discoveries show that within Africa, at a later time than anyone had ever guessed, a remarkably primitive hominin species still survived. Maybe *naledi* evolved from an early form of *Homo erectus.* Or maybe an early form of *naledi* really did exist much earlier, before *erectus,* and gave rise to both our much later *naledi* fossils and other forms of *Homo,* even modern humans. We cannot rule out anything at this point: The anatomical mosaic of *naledi*'s skeleton makes it hard to be sure exactly where it fits on our family tree. If there's one thing that the Rising Star discoveries tell us, it is that we haven't found everything that's out there. That's what an explorer wants to hear.

The species we call *Homo sapiens*—modern humans—includes everyone living in the world today. Archaic forms of humans, like *Homo erectus* or Neanderthals, no longer exist. How did that happen? Sometime before 200,000 years ago, an African population of humans began to grow in numbers. This population gave rise to more than 90 percent of the genetic ancestry of people living now throughout the world—but it's not clear exactly who that population of ancestral people were.

Four known fossil specimens from Africa share a basic skull shape with living people—three from Ethiopia that are more than 150,000 years old, and one from Tanzania that is a bit younger. That much we can observe, but we really don't know if those fossils represent the direct ancestors of the special population from which we all arose—or their cousins. Each of those fossils shares some similarities with modern humans, and yet they are much more different from one another than anyone alive in the planet is today. We have evolved a lot since that time, making it hard to tell which hominin fossils, if any, might be our direct ancestors. And when we look back even further in time, into the time of *naledi*, no fossil remains look very similar to modern humans.

In the last few years, DNA evidence has added tremendous complexity to our understanding of this story of modern humans. Genetic testing shows us that when one tiny branch of the modern human species first migrated out of Africa, they encountered some of their archaic cousins—the Neanderthals and Denisovans. Those species interbred, scattering a small percentage of Neanderthal and Denisovan genetic ancestry through much of the human population. Meanwhile, Africa remained the center of our origins, and—as we continue to discover—within the huge diversity of African environments lived other distant archaic cousins. The fossil record of Africa is so sparse that we have no idea who these distant cousins may have been. But inside the genomes of living African populations, we see traces of DNA interlaced from unknown populations. The origin of our human species now looks like a braided stream. Branches formed and flowed separately for some distance before they merged again with the growing river as it flowed on to today.

Which brings us back to the mystery of *Homo naledi*. We have now discovered the largest sample of fossils on the continent, representing a species never known before. We have determined that it lived only a few hundred thousand years ago, and we suspect that it may have engaged in deliberate body disposal. These two facts are astounding in themselves, but they raise much larger questions. In the midst of such a diverse continent, what was the place of this unexpected species? Could it have interbred with other populations? Might its DNA have merged into the stream of our own origins?

One comparison is Flores, where a tiny, small-brained species may have been living when modern humans arrived there no earlier than 50,000 years ago. In one way, the Flores discoveries showed that surprises might be in store for us in unexpected places—a revelation we have echoed now in South Africa. But in another way the Flores story confirmed a stereotype about *Homo sapiens,* and that is that humans are fierce competitors. Even small groups of human hunter-gatherers can kill dangerous predators, dominate landscapes, and consume nearly every edible food source. According to conventional thinking, a different hominin population like the Flores hobbits might evolve in isolation, but once large-brained humans arrived on the scene, that isolated species was doomed. So much of the bitter fight about *H. floresiensis* arose from this assumption: Many scientists could not imagine how a small-brained species could survive when the larger-brained human species was in the picture.

Looking at *naledi* we have to throw away this stereotype. This species was not isolated on an island. It lived smack in the heartland of human origins. *Naledi* was not small and dwarfed: It was the size of modern hunter-gatherers, with hips, legs, and feet apparently as well made for walking as those of modern humans. Its teeth show that it likely relied upon meat and other high-energy foods; its hands and fingers show the capability to make almost any kind of stone tool; and despite its small brain, it appears to have developed some very interesting behaviors. *Naledi* did not survive by being safely isolated, and its anatomy gives us no reason to think it avoided competition for the same resources as larger-brained human species. *Naledi* did not survive merely by being different. In some ways, at least, *naledi* could only have survived by being better.

What does all this mean? We need to look at the dawn of modern human behavior in a new way. Conventional theories tell us that African technology in the last 400,000 years followed a slow, gradual progression. First some groups of ancient hominin toolmakers moved from hand axes and chopping tools toward more deadly spear points and complicated flaking methods. Somebody started to dabble in pigment, and to travel longer distances to seek out useful stones to bring home. By 70,000 years ago, some African peoples were making objects that communicated information and took on value as symbols, like inscribed ostrich eggshells and shell beads.

Archaeologists have assumed that all the people who took these great steps in human development were direct ancestors of modern *Homo sapiens*—that human evolution happened in a single straight line. But how do we know?

*Naledi* shows us how incomplete this idea must be. Imagine the possibility: Several hundreds of thousands of years ago, another species was out there with its own society and social behaviors. It was very different from modern humans, but it was clever and capable of making things. Granted, no tools have yet been found with the bones of *naledi*—but no tools have been found in close contact with any other hominin bones from around the same time period. We simply cannot assume who was making the artifacts we have found.

We are only at the beginning stages of learning about this remarkable species. These discoveries force us to ask new questions and to question old assumptions. Right now we can only speculate how the larger story will fit together as we continue to find more evidence and test new hypotheses. So much of Africa remains almost entirely unexplored.

Very likely there are more early hominin species to be discovered. We would be foolish to assume that *naledi* was the only one that has been hidden. If we stop connecting the dots, assuming evolutionary change happens in a straight line, and open up to larger possibilities, we can see that at the time of the dawn of modern humankind, Africa was full of different traditions, each one diverse and reflecting an accumulation of learning over thousands of generations. One of these traditions may have belonged to the ancestors of the first modern humans, but we don't know which, or where they may have lived. Another tradition, maybe several, must have been made by species like *naledi*. Maybe our ancestors could draw upon many traditions, learning not only from parents and grandparents but also from distant cousins—like *naledi*.

# EPILOGUE

JOHN HAWKS
NEAR JOHANNESBURG, 2016

"You want to see something interesting?"

After working with Lee Berger for a couple of years, I was no longer easily surprised. When enough hominin fossil discoveries take you in unexpected directions, you learn to go with the flow.

This morning's little field trip had started like many others, a predawn drive from Johannesburg out to the Cradle, the mid-July winter sunrise just hitting us as we left the northern outskirts of the city. We were heading out with Kevin Hand, a friend of Lee's and a scientist at the Jet Propulsion Laboratory in Pasadena, California. Kevin had given a guest lecture the day before. Beating the traffic gave some time for breakfast, and we talked about the discoveries of the past few years before heading out to the field.

On most excursions like this, Malapa is the star of the program. The Nash trust had renamed the expansive property the Malapa Nature Reserve, and it was always an enjoyable excursion, driving out over the grassland with its stock of animals, Lee's Jeep bouncing over the rocky trails and splashing through the stream at the bottom of the valley. Now that a protective structure had been completed, crouching impressively over the little site, archaeologists were resuming their work, clearing and surveying the ground surface around the breccia deposit. The team had already made new discoveries—

fossils embedded in blocks of breccia that had been blasted clear of the site or used to fill the miners' track. Soon they would be excavating new blocks to recover the rest of the first two *sediba* skeletons, and we expected to find additional pieces of hominin individuals that a few new fragments promised. Those discoveries would take time to prepare out of the breccia, and Lee had arranged a preparation lab at the Maropeng visitors center—20 miles away—to allow people to watch the process as preparators scribed these new fossils out of the blocks of breccia. From the CT scans of the blocks, we knew some of the fossils that the team would soon see, and we planned to let some of them remain in their rocky prisons, waiting for future technology that might uncover new secrets. Still, every time we walked around the site, we wondered what unexpected discoveries might remain in the rock.

From the outside, the Rising Star site is much less impressive than Malapa—an eaten-down horse pasture and an unimpressive cave opening. Without donning caving gear and descending, visitors cannot see anything but the entrance cut into the dolomite hillside. Lee's foundation had started work to purchase the property and place it in a public interest trust, protecting the site forever, but the hard work of rehabilitating the property and establishing a proper field station remained in the future. The area around the cave wasn't as pretty as Malapa, but it had a hold on me. I had as good an idea as anyone alive what waited here deep underground, and with all I knew, I still couldn't answer the most interesting questions.

Lee pulled his Jeep off the road at a different spot, however—not Malapa and not the Rising Star opening I thought we were going to see. "I want to stop off and look at this new site the guys found," he said. "Here, take a flashlight."

A few minutes of walking brought us to the solid rock edge of a deep pit with steeply sloped walls and trees growing up from the bottom. In the far wall of the pit was a dark opening with the look of a miner's old work.

"I can't believe I didn't see this before," Lee said as he led us down the steep incline. I paused to find a footing, gripping a sapling as I skidded down the moss-covered rock. The pit was like an ancient amphitheater, its floor littered with fractured limestone and breccia, with an enormous boulder seemingly suspended in mid-slide. Tree roots snaked along the face of the rock as we moved farther down. Along one face, we moved next to a solid breccia wall flecked with cross sections of fossil bones. Kevin followed Lee closely, but I dawdled, my attention fixed on the wall. Any one of those fossils might be the next discovery, I thought. After all, how many expert anatomists had come down this same slope?

Well, I knew one, and he was striding ahead of me.

Lee stopped at the cave entrance, pulling a flashlight from a pouch at his hip and flicking it on. He led us into the darkness. Inside, the walls opened into an enormous cavern. We studied the walls carefully, breccia deposits covering some of them. We made our way around an enormous debris pile left behind after the mining activity—huge chunks of dolomite blasted from the ceiling. Lee's path trended to the opposite side of the cavern, where a shaft of daylight came from the cave roof above. Kevin and I fanned out, studying the cave walls and beaming our flashlights into every corner.

As I scanned the darkness, my mind wandered over all that had happened during the past few years. *Sediba* had brought me to South Africa to work, and then I was caught up in the Rising Star expedition. I became involved because these discoveries were changing the science. The *sediba* fossils made us all realize that there was new evidence of our evolution out there, waiting for us to find it. Rising Star fulfilled that promise, the largest hominin discovery in Africa and a new species at that, hidden within one of the most explored regions in the world. Who knows what will come next?

So now here I was, shining a light into the dark vastness of this uncharted cave.

"You want to look at this?" Lee stood within the beam of sunlight, smiling and holding out a fist-size rock. As I came closer, I didn't see anything all that obviously special about it. Had he found a stone core left behind by some ancient toolmakers?

I took the rock from his outstretched hands, carefully turning it over to inspect it. Two teeth caught my eye, each the size of a nickel. The bone of the jaw that contained them was light cream in color, strong and robustly built, perfectly in proportion for the large teeth. I glanced up at Lee, who simply stood watching me examine the ancient hominin jaw, an amused look on his face.

I said what we were all thinking: "Here we go again."

# Project Participants, 2008–2015

## Underground Astronauts

Marina Elliott
Elen Feuerriegel

Alia Gurtov
K. Lindsay (Eaves) Hunter

Hannah Morris
Becca Peixotto

## Field and Laboratory Staff

Pedro Boshoff
Wayne Crichton
Bonita de Klerk
Nompumelelo Hlophe
Rick Hunter
Meshack Kgasi
Roseberry Laguza
Wilma Lawrence
Boy Louw

Justin Makanku
Irene Maphosa
Danny Mithi
Zandile Ndaba
Bongani Nkosi
Mduduzi Nyalunga
Wilhelmina Pretorius
Maropeng Ramalepa
Sonia Sequeira

Mathabela Tsikoane
Steven Tucker
Dirk van Rooyen
Renier van der Merwe
Merill van der Walt
Michael Wall
Celeste Yates

## Volunteer Cavers

Megan Berger
Matthew Berger
Leon de Kock
Bruce Dickie
John Dickie
Matthew Dickie
Selena Dickie
Andre Doussy

Jeremy Grey
Allen Herweg
Michael Herweg
Dave Ingold
Greg Justus
Peter Kenyon
Irene Kruger
Lindin Mazillis

Gerrie Pretorius
Colin Redmayne-Smith
Sharron Reynolds
Christo Saayman
Rupert Stander
Pieter Theron
Veronica van der Schyff

## Researchers

Tamiru Abiye
Rebecca Ackermann
Lucinda Backwell
Marion Bamford
Markus Bastir
George Belyanin
Jackie Berger
Lee Berger
Barry Bogin

Debra Bolter
Juliet Brophy
Noël Cameron
Keely Carlson
Kristian Carlson
Guy Charlesworth
Steven Churchill
Zachary Cofran
Kerri Collins

Kimberly Congdon
Darryl de Ruiter
Jeremy DeSilva
Thomas DeWitt
Andrew Deane
Lucas Delezene
Mana Dembo
Paul Dirks
Michelle Drapeau

Marina Elliott
Daniel Farber
Elen Feuerriegel
Ryan Franklin
Nakita Frater
Daniel Garcia-Martínez
Heather Garvin
David Green
Debbie Guatelli-Steinberg
Alia Gurtov
William Harcourt-Smith
James Harrison
Adam Hartstone-Rose
John Hawks
John Hellstrom
Amanda Henry
Andy Herries
Trenton Holliday
Kenneth Holt
Joel Irish
Tea Jashashvili
Zubair Jinnah
Rachelle Keeling
Job Kibii
Robert Kidd
Geoffrey King
Tracy Kivell
Jan Kramers
Ashley Kruger

Brian Kuhn
Rodrigo Lacruz
Myra Laird
Julia Lee-Thorp
Scott Legge
Marisa Macias
Vincent Makhubela
Damiano Marchi
Sandra Mathews
Anne-Sophie Meriaux
Marc Meyer
Yusavia Moodley
Tshegofatso Mophatlane
Charles Musiba
Shahed Nalla
Lucia Ndlovu
Enquye Negash
Frank Neumann
Edward Odes
Caley Orr
Kelly Ostrofsky
Benjamin Passey
Lucille Pereira
Robyn Pickering
Davorka Radovčić
Patrick
Randolph-Quinney
Nichelle Reed
Mike Richards

Eric Roberts
Lloyd Rossouw
Paul Sandberg
Peter Schmid
Lauren Schroeder
Jill Scott
Louis Scott
Matthew Skinner
Tanya Smith
Tawnee Sparling
Matt Sponheimer
Christine Steininger
Dietrich Stout
Paul Tafforeau
Phillip Taru
Mirriam Tawane
Francis Thackeray
Zach Throckmorton
Matthew Tocheri
Peter Ungar
Aurore Val
Caroline VanSickle
Christopher Walker
Pianpian Wei
Eveline Weissen
Lars Werdelin
Scott Williams
Jon Woodhead
Bernhard Zipfel

## National Geographic Staff

John Cullum
Andrew Howley

# BIBLIOGRAPHY

Antón, Susan C., Richard Potts, and Leslie C. Aiello. "Evolution of early *Homo:* An integrated biological perspective." *Science* 345, no. 6192 (2014): 1236828.

Balter, Michael. " 'Hobbit' bones go home to Jakarta." *Science* 307 (2005): 1386.

Berger, L. R. *Functional morphology of the hominoid shoulder, past and present* (doctoral dissertation). University of the Witwatersrand, 1994.

Berger, L. R. "The mosaic nature of *Australopithecus sediba.*" *Science* 340, no. 6129 (2013): 163–65.

Berger, L. R., and M. Aronson. *The skull in the rock: How a scientist, a boy, and Google Earth opened a new window on human origins.* National Geographic Press, 2012.

Berger, L. R., and J. Brink. "Late Middle Pleistocene fossils, including a human patella, from the Riet River gravels, Free State, South Africa." *South African Journal of Science* 92 (1996): 277–78.

Berger, L. R., and R. J. Clarke. "Eagle involvement in accumulation of the Taung Child fauna." *Journal of Human Evolution* 29, no. 3 (1995): 275–99.

Berger, L. R., and B. Hilton-Barber. *In the footsteps of eve: The mystery of human origins.* National Geographic Society, Adventure Press, 2000.

Berger, L. R., and R. Lacruz. "Preliminary report on the first excavations at the new fossil site of Motsetse, Gauteng, South Africa." *South African Journal of Science* 99 (2003): 279–82.

Berger, L. R., and J. E. Parkington. "A new Pleistocene hominid-bearing locality at Hoedjiespunt, South Africa." *American Journal of Physical Anthropology* 98, no. 4 (1995): 601–09.

Berger, L. R., A. W. Keyser, and P. V. Tobias. "Gladysvale: First early hominid site discovered in South Africa since 1948." *American Journal of Physical Anthropology* 92, no. 1 (1993): 107–11.

Berger, L. R., W. Liu, and X. Wu. "Investigation of a credible report by a U. S. Marine on the location of the missing Peking Man fossils." *South African Journal of Science* 108, no. 3–4 (2012): 6–8.

Berger, L. R., et al. "*Australopithecus sediba:* A new species of *Homo*-like australopith from South Africa." *Science* 328, no. 5975 (2010): 195–204.

Berger, L. R., et al. "*Homo naledi,* a new species of the genus *Homo* from the Dinaledi Chamber, South Africa." *eLife* 4 (2015): e09560.

Berger, L. R., et al. "A Mid-Pleistocene in situ fossil brown hyaena *(Parahyaena brunnea)* latrine from Gladysvale Cave, South Africa." *Palaeogeography, Palaeoclimatology, Palaeoecology* 279, no. 3 (2009): 131–36.

Berger, L. R., et al. "Small-bodied humans from Palau, Micronesia." *PLOS ONE* 3, no. 3 (2008): e1780.

Brophy, J. K., et al. "Preliminary investigation of the new Middle Stone Age site of Plovers Lake, South Africa." *Current Research in the Pleistocene* 23 (2006): 41–43.

Brown, P., et al. "A new small-bodied hominin from the late Pleistocene of Flores, Indonesia." *Nature* 431, no. 7012 (2004): 1055–61.

Carlson, K. J., et al. "The endocast of MH1, *Australopithecus sediba*." *Science* 333, no. 6048 (2011): 1402–07.

Churchill, S., L. R. Berger, and J. P. Parkington. "A *Homo* cf. *heidelbergensis* tibia from the Hoedjiespunt site, Western Cape, South Africa." *South African Journal of Science* 96 (2000): 367–68.

Churchill, S. E., et al. "The upper limb of *Australopithecus sediba*." *Science* 340, no. 6129 (2013): 1233477.

Dalton, R. "Pacific 'dwarf' bones cause controversy." *Nature* 452 (2008): 133. Available online at www.nature.com/news/2008/080310/full/452133a.html.

de Ruiter, D. J., and L. R. Berger. "Leopard (*Panthera pardus* Linneaus) cave caching related to anti-theft behaviour in the John Nash Nature Reserve, South Africa." *African Journal of Ecology* 39, no. 4 (2001): 396–98.

de Ruiter, D. J., and L. R. Berger. "Leopards as taphonomic agents in dolomitic caves: Implications for bone accumulations in the hominid-bearing deposits of South Africa." *Journal of Archaeological Science* 27, no. 8 (2000): 665–84.

de Ruiter, D. J., et al. "Mandibular remains support taxonomic validity of *Australopithecus sediba*." *Science* 340, no. 6129 (2013): 1232997.

DeSilva, J. M., et al. "The lower limb and mechanics of walking in *Australopithecus sediba*." *Science* 340, no. 6129 (2013): 1232999.

Dirks, P. H., et al. "Geological setting and age of *Australopithecus sediba* from southern Africa." *Science* 328, no. 5975 (2010): 205–08.

Dirks P., et al. "Geological and taphonomic context for the new hominin species *Homo naledi* from the Dinaledi Chamber, South Africa." *eLife* 4 (2015): e09561.

Gabunia, L., and A. A. Vekua. "Plio-Pleistocene hominid from Dmanisi, East Georgia, Caucasus." *Nature* 373, no. 6514 (1995): 509–12.

Gibbons, A. "Anthropological Casting Call." *Science* (2012). Available online at sciencemag.org/news/2012/04/anthropological-casting-call.

Hartstone-Rose, A., et al. "The Plio-Pleistocene ancestor of wild dogs, *Lycaon sekowei* n. sp." *Journal of Paleontology* 84, no. 2 (2010): 299–308.

Henry, A. G., et al. "The diet of *Australopithecus sediba*." *Nature* 487, no. 7405 (2012): 90–93.

Hughes, A. R., and P. V. Tobias. "A fossil skull probably of the genus *Homo* from Sterkfontein, Transvaal." *Nature* 265, no. 5592 (1977): 310–12.

Irish, J. D., et al. "Dental morphology and the phylogenetic 'place' of *Australopithecus sediba*." *Science* 340, no. 6129 (2013): 1233062.

Johanson, D., and M. A. Edey. *Lucy: The beginnings of humankind*. Simon and Schuster, 1981.

Keyser, A. W., et al. "Drimolen: A new hominid-bearing site in Gauteng, South Africa." *South African Journal of Science* 96, no. 4 (2000): 193–97.

Kibii, J. M., et al. "A partial pelvis of *Australopithecus sediba*." *Science* 333, no. 6048 (2011): 1407–11.

Kimbel, W. H. "Palaeoanthropology: Hesitation on hominin history." *Nature* 497, no. 7451 (2013): 573–74.

Kivell, T. L., et al. "*Australopithecus sediba* hand demonstrates mosaic evolution of locomotor and manipulative abilities." *Science* 333, no. 6048 (2011): 1411–17.

Leakey, L. S., P. V. Tobias, and J. R. Napier. "A new species of the genus *Homo* from Olduvai Gorge." *Nature* 202 (1964): 7–9.

McGraw, W. S., and L. R. Berger. "Raptors and primate evolution." *Evolutionary Anthropology: Issues, News, and Reviews* 22, no. 6 (2013): 280–93.

McHenry, H. M., and L. R. Berger. "Body proportions in *Australopithecus afarensis* and *A. africanus* and the origin of the genus *Homo*." *Journal of Human Evolution* 35, no. 1 (1998): 1–22.

McHenry, H. M., and L. R. Berger. "Limb lengths in *Australopithecus* and the origin of the genus *Homo*." *South African Journal of Science* 94, no. 9 (1998): 447–50.

Morell, V. *Ancestral passions: The Leakey family and the quest for humankind's beginnings.* Simon and Schuster, 2011.

Mutter, R. J., L. R. Berger, and P. Schmid. "New evidence of the giant hyaena, *Pachycrocuta brevirostris* (Carnivora, Hyaenidae), from the Gladysvale Cave Deposit (Plio-Pleistocene, John Nash Nature Reserve, Gauteng, South Africa)." *Palaeontologia Africana* 37 (2001): 103–13.

Pickering, R., et al. "*Australopithecus sediba* at 1.977 Ma and implications for the origins of the genus *Homo*." *Science* 333, no. 6048 (2011): 1421–23.

Roberts, D., and L. R. Berger. "Last interglacial (c. 117 Kyr) human footprints from South Africa." *South African Journal of Science* 93 (1997): 349–50.

Schmid, P., and L. R. Berger. "Middle Pleistocene hominid carpal proximal phalanx from the Gladysvale site, South Africa." *South African Journal of Science* 93, no. 10 (1997): 430–31.

Schmid, P., et al. "Mosaic morphology in the thorax of *Australopithecus sediba*." *Science* 340, no. 6129 (2013): 1234598.

Spoor, Fred. "Palaeoanthropology: Malapa and the genus *Homo*." *Nature* 478, no. 7367 (2011): 44–45.

Stynder, D. D., et al. "Human mandibular incisors from the late Middle Pleistocene locality of Hoedjiespunt 1, South Africa." *Journal of Human Evolution* 41, no. 5 (2001): 369–83.

Tobias, P. V. *Into the Past: A Memoir*. Picador Africa, 2005.

Tobias, P. V. "When and by whom was the Taung skull discovered?" In *Para conocer al hombre: homenaje a Santiago Genovése*. Mexico City: Universidad Nacional Autonoma da Mexico (1990): 207–13.

Tobias, P. V. *Olduvai Gorge. Vol. 2. The cranium and maxillary dentition of* Australopithecus (Zinjanthropus) boisei. Cambridge University Press, 1967.

Weber, G. W. "Virtual anthropology (VA): A call for glasnost in paleoanthropology." *Anatomical Record* 265, no. 4 (2001): 193–201.

White T. D. "A view on the science: Physical anthropology at the millennium." *American Journal of Physical Anthropology* 113 (2000): 287–92.

White, T. D., et al. "*Ardipithecus ramidus* and the paleobiology of early hominids." *Science* 326, no. 5949 (2009): 64–86.

Williams, S. A., et al. "The vertebral column of *Australopithecus sediba*." *Science* 340, no. 6129 (2013): 1232996.

Zipfel, B., and L. R. Berger. "New Cenozoic fossil-bearing site abbreviations for the collections of the University of the Witwatersrand." *Palaeontologia africana* 44 (2009): 77–81.

Zipfel, B., et al. "The foot and ankle of *Australopithecus sediba*." *Science* 333, no. 6048 (2011): 1417–20.

# INDEX

Berger, Megan 17, 111, 145
Bird, Garrreth 132
Bishop, Gale 29
Body disposal, deliberate 163, 204–206, 215–216, 220
Boshoff, Pedro 107–111, 113, 115, 116, 118, 120, 138
Botswana: survey 49
Broom, Robert 34, 35, 36, 44, 84
Brown, Peter 57
Buxton Limeworks, Taung, South Africa: fossil finds 32–33

**C**

Calcite 14, 89, 102, 152
Calcium 72, 203
Calcium carbonate 199
Cameron, James 119, 120
Carbon dioxide 119, 151, 153
Carlson, Kristian 82
Chert 201
Chimpanzees
  ancestors 43
  emotions 205
  first metacarpal **156**
  heel 94
  trapezoid bone 191
Churchill , Steve 48, 61, 77, 119, 133, 152, 156, 167, 196
Clades 94, 95
Clarke, Ron 52–54
Collagen 203
Cooper's Cave, South Africa 13
Cradle of Humankind World Heritage site, South Africa 11–16, 77, 152, 160, 183, 197, 201, 202

management authority 124
visitors center 210, 224
  *see also* Cooper's Cave; Gladysvale Cave; Malapa; Motsetse; Rising Star; Sterkfontein; Swartkrans
Cro-Magnons 32
Crystals 89, 182, 217
CT scanners 86–87
Cullum, John 132

**D**

Dart, Raymond 32–36, 38, 44, 54–55, 75, 183, 188
Darwin, Charles 33, 34, 94
Dating methods 39, 89, 181, 182–183
De Klerk, Bonita 108
De Ruiter, Darryl 77, 119, 167
"Dear Boy." *see Zinjanthropus boisei*
Denisovans 219
Diamond mining 108
Dickie, John 113, 133, 134, 137
Dinosaurs 21, 23, 28, 29
Dirks, Paul 77, 81, 89, 181, 200
Ditsong Museum, Pretoria, South Africa 202
Dmanisi, Republic of Georgia: skulls **194,** 194–195
DNA (deoxyribonucleic acid) 43, 45, 209, 219–220
Documentary filmmaking 62–64
Drimolen, South Africa 108
Dube, Charlton 69, 74, 75

**E**

East Africa 36–41, 51, 52, 83, 89, 91; *see also* Ethiopia; Kenya; Tanzania
Edey, Maitland 28
Electron spin resonance (ESR) 182, 217, 218
eLife (journal) 208–209
Elliott, Marina 127–128, 143–151, 155, 161, 166, 171–172, 176, 190, 211–215
Endocasts 32–33, **33**
Ethiopia
  fossil specimens 46, 184, 219
  government 51
  *see also* Afar region; Hadar; Middle Awash; Omo Valley
Europe
  Cro-Magnons 32
  Neanderthals 32, 34
  scientific access to fossils 59

**F**

Facebook 124–125, 126, 132, 174–175
Fall line 28
Feuerriegel, Elen 127, 128, 155, 160, 214
Fire, use of 35, 58, 205
Flores (island), Indonesia 57–60, 62–63, 220; *see also Homo floresiensis*
Flowstone analysis 80, 89–90, 182, 217
Footprints, fossil 40, 48

**G**

Garcia, Terry 118
Garvin, Heather 193
Genetic discoveries 45

# ABOUT THE AUTHORS

**Lee Berger** is a research professor at the Evolutionary Studies Institute at the University of the Witwatersrand in South Africa and an explorer-in-residence at the National Geographic Society. An award-winning researcher, author, and speaker, Berger, in 1997, was the first recipient of the National Geographic Society's Prize for Research and Exploration. In 2016 he was named the Rolex National Geographic Explorer of the Year, and that same year *Time* magazine identified him as one of the 100 most influential people in the world. His previous books include *In the Footsteps of Eve* and *The Skull in the Rock*. He lives in Johannesburg, South Africa, with his wife and two children.

**John Hawks** is the Vilas-Borghesi Distinguished Achievement Professor of Anthropology at the University of Wisconsin–Madison, where he recently received the H. I. Romnes Faculty Fellowship and its Vilas Associate Award. He worked with Lee Berger during the Rising Star expedition and on subsequent fossil description and analysis. He maintains *johnhawks.net,* a weblog on paleoanthropology, genetics, and evolution. He lives in Madison, Wisconsin, with his wife and four children.

# ILLUSTRATIONS CREDITS

ORIGINAL ART BY JOHN Hawks. Cover, Robert Clark; Jacket Flap, Brett Eloff, Courtesy of the University of the Witwatersrand; Insert 1: 1, Brent Stirton/Getty Images Reportage; 2 (UP), Courtesy of Lee Berger; 2 (LO), Courtesy of Lee Berger; 3, Brent Stirton/ Getty Images Reportage; 4, Courtesy of the University of the Witwatersrand; 5, Courtesy of the University of the Witwatersrand; 6, Brent Stirton, Courtesy of the University of the Witwatersrand; 7, Brett Eloff, Courtesy of the University of the Witwatersrand; 8, Courtesy of the University of the Witwatersrand; 9, Ismael MonteroVerdu, Courtesy of the ESRF and the University of the Witwatersrand; 10, Ismael MonteroVerdu, Courtesy of the ESRF and the University of the Witwatersrand; 11, Brett Eloff, Courtesy of the University of the Witwatersrand; 12, John Gurche/National Geographic Creative; 13, Brett Eloff, Courtesy of the University of the Witwatersrand; 14, Brett Eloff, Courtesy of the University of the Witwatersrand; 15, John Gurche/National Geographic Creative; 16, John Gurche; Insert 2: 1, Courtesy of John Hawks; 2, Ashley Kruger; 3 (UP), Herman Verwey/Foto24/Gallo Images/Getty Images; 3 (LO), Robert Clark; 4, Robert Clark; 5 (UP), Robert Clark; 5 (LO), Elliot Ross; 6, Garrreth Bird; 7, Rachelle Keeling; 8, Courtesy of John Hawks; 9, Robert Clark; 10, Peter Schmid; 11, Courtesy of John Hawks; 12, Courtesy of John Hawks; 13, Robert Clark; 14, John Gurche; 15, Courtesy of John Hawks; 16, Jon Foster/National Geographic Creative.